THE
SEVEN
PROMISES
OF
HOPE

By

Jan McKenzie

PUBLISHED BY:
Jan McKenzie
Norcross, GA 30071
janmckenzie@yourhopegrows.com

ISBN-13: 978-0615565903

ISBN-10: 0615565905

ACKNOWLEDGEMENTS

So many thanks, so little time. First, I give my heartfelt gratitude to my daughter Jessica, who is helpful and wise beyond her years. I so appreciate your listening ear, insightful feedback, and hard work in setting up our first website, social media and more. No mother could ever ask for a better daughter. Steve and Linda Short and Debbie Thomas have been the most faithful prayer partners this side of heaven and a rock for my sometimes weary heart and hands. My deepest thanks to Susan Lorek and Jane Edgar, who have been at the heart of envisioning how to get this book to those who will hopefully love and benefit from it. They also provided insight, help and encouragement during the process of its creation in more ways than I can list here. Hugh Eaton taught me a lot about the skill of writing while engaged in his own big story out in Colorado. Thanks, Hugh. I'm grateful for my sister Mundy, my son Josh, and the innumerable others who have listened to my stories as I read, re-read, and read to them again, both over the phone and in person. Every storyteller needs a willing audience.

For every word of encouragement, every great idea, every prayer, and the power of your combined brilliance, I am deeply grateful. Each of you exemplifies love in action.

To the many people whose stories are told here, I am also grateful. Thanks for sharing your tales—both the pain and the power—for your stories demonstrate why each of us has reason to hope.

TABLE OF CONTENTS

TABLE OF CONTENTS

INTRODUCTION

It was an ordinary day in many ways. I had just finished setting up the room where I would be teaching a small group of business leaders that afternoon. The Wall Street Journal was on the desk in front of me, rumpled from where I had scanned it while grabbing a bite to eat. For the past few months it was easy to find examples of poor leadership in its pages, leadership that had shipwrecked not only companies but whole economies. The stories made great fodder for our classroom discussions.

Maybe it was the reading that stimulated my thoughts. Maybe it was just one of those days—with the right barometric pressure and a cloud cover that tugged at my emotions. Whatever the reason, I found myself thinking about the "greats" in business leadership and learning. I recalled the people who deeply influenced what I taught our associates and leaders. These experts had a special way of introducing people to new ways of thinking and doing.

As I was considering those on my list, I realized that each of them had a theme they returned to over and over. One was passionate about teamwork and the dysfunctions that were barriers to it. A favorite of mine, whose focus was on leadership, provided a "situational" model so practical and helpful that I taught it to almost everyone in our company. Another had a heart for integrity and the habits of those who want to be highly effective in their lives. Each of their books reflected a part of their core theme, the "heart" of their message that struck a passionate and lasting chord in them.

"What about me?" I thought unexpectedly. "Is there a theme in my life? Is there something that has resurfaced in my heart over the years? What evokes my passion and fuels my work?"

The answer came to me instantly. Hope. I realized at that moment that hope was the theme of my life.

I had discovered hope while puzzling over the broken pieces of my own life as well as the lives of friends, family and even strangers. Like an emotional x-ray, hope revealed to me the patterns woven from seemingly disparate events. Maybe because I needed hope so often myself and found its power during some hard times of my own, I was passionate about sharing it with others.

Hope is also the lifeblood of what I do professionally—teach. It takes hope to believe that people who have been through the formative stages of life come to our classrooms and not only take away new ideas and ways of working but also apply these. I trusted that despite inertia, lifelong habits, individual personalities and the scars of life working against what we teach, our training made a positive difference for our students.

On a personal level, I've spent my days off for the past few years writing about moments when I and others have found hope unexpectedly. Thinking back to these stories I wondered if there were patterns to what I had witnessed and written. Was there something in these accounts that translated into a few real and useful truths about hope and its power?

With only a few minutes before leaders from all over the company came streaming in, the patterns of hope took shape in my mind. Grabbing a piece of paper I began to write. I saw that the events in the stories I'd experienced, witnessed and written about did indeed fall into recognizable categories. The results of each story were not random but represented some truth about hope that could help me to better understand its power. That is how The Seven Promises of Hope were born—on a piece of scratch paper, in the middle of a crowded day, in a room on the eighth floor while I was waiting to teach. As I have worked with these promises and thought about them over time, each one has emerged more completely.

This book is not a theological treatise on hope. I leave that to those who are much more qualified and learned than I. It is not a research document, although some might argue that life itself is the research that teaches us the most. Rather, this book is filled with true accounts of what happens when hope comes to life. Every chapter defines one of the Seven Promises and demonstrates the promise through the stories of real people, events and animals in the sometimes simple, sometimes fantastic moments of their lives.

Your story is in here, you know. What makes me think so? All of us have hoped at some point in our lives. Whether in simple or desperate situations, we have all hoped for something we wanted or needed. Most of us have hoped for something that didn't work out the way we expected. Some of us became disenchanted in the process. That is true in many of the stories in this book as well but because of hope, those disappointments aren't the end. When you learn how hope works, you learn about its power to change more than just situations. The real promise of hope is its ability to transform not only our circumstances but also our hearts.

I'm surer now than ever that there are reasons to hope and that even when deferred, hope springs to life in the most unexpected times and places.

Let the Hope begin.

THE TOP THREE

*"But for right now, until that completeness, we have three things to do to lead us toward that consummation: **Trust** steadily in God, **hope** unswervingly, **love** extravagantly. And the best of the three is love."*
1 Corinthians 13:13 the Message

Faith, hope and love—these are familiar words for most of us.

Faith is the cornerstone of knowing God, the electricity in the wiring that connects us to Him. The Bible says that it is impossible to please God without faith. It is pretty much a benchmark of our experience with Him.

I learned about faith when I was nineteen years old, in an unfamiliar city with strangers I would never see again. Contrary to my own preconceived notions of who God was, I was swept away by the overwhelming sense that God loved me and that Jesus was real. I can't even say that I "accepted" Him at that moment, for it didn't seem to be something that I *did* as much as something that came over me.

"Jesus loves you," said the stranger, after responding to some questions I asked him that had rusted shut my heart against both the man Jesus and the religious structures that surrounded Him.

Have you ever had questions like that about how this God thing works? The questions all seem to end up coming down to something like this: If God, then why? You can fill in the blank. If God is real, then why do bad things happen? If God loves us, then why is there suffering? There are quite a few variations on the theme. If I remember correctly, I was concerned with Christ's

11

presence, or my perceived lack of it, in lands far away. I was particularly concerned about India.

I don't remember exactly what this stranger said to dispel my doubts long enough for God to touch my heart. I believe he suggested that if I wasn't actually in India to witness what was going on, maybe I didn't really know what Jesus was doing there. A few years later Mother Teresa showed up on the scene, lending some validity to his point. I'd say I let go of my doubts at that moment, but it was more like they were very old manuscripts suddenly exposed to bright light. They just kind of crumbled, like the mummy who turns to sand in the scary movies.

I knew when this stranger spoke to me that the love he shared was true. I was surprised by this intervention of God's love, in particular because Jesus was at the center of it. My early life experience with church and religion had convinced me that Jesus was no more than a name with a list of rules attached. In my search for God, Jesus wasn't even on my list of possibilities. So the fact that I experienced Him there in Jacksonville, Florida while waiting for friends delayed from another city was unexpected to say the least. This was the beginning of faith for me. It wasn't until later that I understood the meaning of words like redemption and grace.

Over time I began to understand the idea that it is "by **grace** you have been saved, **through faith**—and this is not from yourselves, it is the gift of God," (Ephesians 2:7-9, NIV.) In other words, it is not something we accomplish on our own, but rather simple faith initiated by a loving God that brings us to Him.

Faith is a cornerstone, the bridge that connects us to God and the first listed in God's famous "top three" attributes—faith, hope and love. We all know the importance of faith.

As for love, volumes have been written about it, our music proclaims the power of its presence, and the Bible makes the bold statement that "God is love." When St. Paul says it is the "greatest of these" (1 Corinthians 13:13)—emphasizing that love is number one on the hit parade of God's greatest melodies—that pretty much sums it up. Jesus displayed the ultimate love when He died for us on a cross, carrying the weight of what we had done wrong so that we could be reconnected with God. Now that's love.

But sandwiched right between these two superstars in God's kingdom lies a personal favorite of mine—hope. Like a middle child it doesn't always get the attention it deserves. First children are the promise of a family's legacy and the youngest represent love given unsparingly. But the middle child has to work for his or her acceptance and recognition. So it is with hope. We know it's there but it's so....well, unsubstantial somehow. I mean compared to faith, which starts and sustains our relationship with God, and love, which represents God himself, hope seems somehow less significant, less weighty. For me it has always felt a little like "faith light," something that in the past I equated with wishes and dreams or childhood desires.

So when did hope become so important, so substantial, in my life? Was it sometime after I realized that the dreams of my youth, my teens, and possibly even my adulthood, just weren't going to pan out the way I had expected? When did life change so that hope became the theme song to my reality show and the one thing that

I could finally see in the dark? At some point, hope was the lens through which I saw my brokenness and the brokenness of others. It gave me the ability to see the worth in that which appeared to be worthless.

Hope steps front and center when there is great pain or peril to overcome.

The singer/songwriter Leonard Cohen says that "there is a crack in everything—that's how the light gets in." [1]

When the cracks in my life became big enough, I began to hope in the light that trickled through and the light that trickled through gave me hope.

So what is hope and how does it work?

Maybe it's easier to talk about what a lack of hope looks like. Martin Luther King Jr. once said, "If you lose hope, somehow you lose the vitality that keeps life moving, you lose the courage to be, that quality that helps you go on in spite of it all."[2] In other words, hope puts fuel in the tank that gives us the energy to keep going. Hope is about possibilities. No matter what things look like today, if we have hope, we believe that someday it can be better. It isn't faith, the knowing and believing that things will be different. It is the thread that ties us to faith, the spark that becomes faith. It is a light in the darkness and an anticipation of goodness.

Vaclav Havel, a former president of the Czech Republic, said "Hope is not the conviction that something will turn out well, but the certainty that something makes sense regardless of how it turns out."[3] This, for me, is an even truer meaning of hope. Hope that is anchored in our circumstances **alone** is bound to disappoint.

I have often asked myself, "In what can I hope?" Is it right to hope that my life will improve or that someone else's will? Or am I only to hope in my eventual, eternal connection with God once this life is left behind? Do I hope, as my friend Chris Rogers says, that "God will get me **out** of my circumstances or that He will get me **through** them?" The answer I'm finding to these questions is "Yes, and." Yes, we hope and then we trust. Keep reading to see how this works in the lives of real people just like you and me.

Also, in my searching I began to see that hope is more than wishing or holding on. It is not what we do when we can't believe, because hope precedes faith. Jon Bevere in his book **Extraordinary** describes hope as "the blueprint and faith as the building materials." Referring to Hebrews 11:1 he quotes, *"Now faith is the substance of things hoped for."* For Jon that means, "If you don't have hope—the vision, picture, image, blueprint in your heart—your faith has nothing to give substance to."[4] Hope provides a plan, faith brings it to life.

Here is the heart of what I have learned—we hope for many reasons. I call these reasons *The 7 Promises of Hope.* They demonstrate why you can and should hope and how it works. They provide a context within which you can understand and be reminded of the power of hope. You can build your hope muscle by understanding these promises and if that muscle has atrophied, you can bring it back to life.

Come discover the territory of hope. It is vast and wondrous and available to all.

THE SEVEN PROMISES OF HOPE

1. We hope because He is Present.

Hope tells us God is present even when we can't see Him.

"So we fix our eyes not on what is seen but on what is unseen. For what is seen is temporary but what is unseen is eternal."
2 Corinthians 4:17-19 NIV

2. We hope in His Purpose.

Hope tells us that God has a purpose for us and that it is good. He is in the business of redeeming the broken and He redeems everything, both good and bad, for His children.

"And we know that God causes all things to work together for good to those who love God, to those who are called according to His purpose."
Romans 8:28 NASB

3. We hope in His Provision.

Hope tells us God will provide "our daily bread," that He will take us to the next step in our journey.

"Don't worry about anything; instead, pray about everything. Tell God what you need, and thank him for all he has done."
Philippians 4:6 NLT

4. We hope in His Participation.

Hope tells us that God meets us where we are—in the everyday moments of our lives.

"O Lord, you have searched me and you know me. You know when I sit and when I rise; you perceive my thoughts from afar. You discern my going out and my lying down; you are familiar with all my ways." Psalm 139: 1-3 NIV

16

5. **Hope grows when we recognize Him in the incomplete Parts of our lives.**

   Hope helps us to recognize God in the incomplete and tells us that we don't have to know the end of the story to see Him in today.

   "I remember my affliction and my wandering, the bitterness and the gall. I well remember them and my soul is downcast within me. Yet this I call to mind and therefore I have hope. Because of the Lord's great love we are not consumed, for his compassions never fail. They are new every morning, great is your faithfulness. I say to myself, "the Lord is my portion. Therefore I will wait for him." The Lord is good to those whose hope is in him, to the one who seeks him." Lamentations 3:19-25 NIV

6. **Hope grows in Patience.**

   Hope tells us to be patient, that God hears our prayers even when he chooses to answer them over time.

   "But hope that is seen is no hope at all. Who hopes for what he already has? But if we hope for what we do not yet have, we wait for it patiently."
   Romans 8:24-25 NIV

7. **Hope grows when our hearts are Pure**.

   Hope grows when we let go of anger and fear. We hope better when we unburden our hearts and believe we are who God says we are, not who others say we are.

   "Blessed are the pure in heart for they will see God."
   Matthew 5:9 NIV

CHAPTER 1

THE FIRST PROMISE OF HOPE: HIS PRESENCE

We hope because He is Present.

Hope tells us that God is present even when we can't see Him.

"So we fix our eyes not on what is seen but on what is unseen. For what is seen is temporary but what is unseen is eternal."

2 Corinthians 4:17-19

RAINED OUT

It's been raining—again. For the past few years we have been in a drought, rationing water in our houses and sprinkling our thirsty lawns only on Tuesdays, Thursdays and every other Sunday. There were times we thought it would never end. The lake that fed the city was so far below its normal level you could walk out several feet into the lakebed and still be on completely dry land. The boat docks sat forlornly on the uncovered earth while water skiing was almost a thing of the past.

All that is over and now we have a different problem. It started raining last spring and it feels like it hasn't stopped since. In September we had what they called a "hundred year flood." I think that means no one alive can remember seeing one that was worse. Bridges were washed out, water rose up past the second floor windows of houses in entire neighborhoods, and roads were completely submerged in various parts of the city.

Now it's January and it's raining again. Not every day but this past weekend the rain started on Saturday morning and continued through Sunday evening. Not the relentless hard rain of September, but steady nevertheless. All that water does something to the landscape. It has all but drowned the grass in my back yard and the silt left by the muddy water has gathered at the bottom of my fence. The flower beds and bushes have wilted, covered in a coat of

Georgia clay. It's just so barren back there. The gardens from previous years are nothing more than a washed out memory.

When I look out over the yard, something in my soul resonates with what I see. There has been too much rain washing away at my spirit lately, too. Physical challenges that simply won't go away have been keeping me from reaching out and doing the things that brighten the landscape of my life. It started like a flood and now, like the steady, slow rain of last weekend, it just keeps pushing back the green areas of my heart.

I've been battling to remember that spring follows winter, dry follows wet, and you can hire people to landscape your yard once the rains stop. I know what I'm looking at is temporary. Just because there has been a setback, it doesn't mean things have to stay that way. Still, it's tempting to take everything at face value, disregarding the possibilities of the future.

When the feelings of loss wash up against my shore, something else echoes in the waves. It is hope. I've been learning to listen to it again. It has taken some time, but I'm listening closely and discovering how to hold on when the rain simply won't let up. As a result, I'm finding the principles of hope that hold true, just as gravity or other natural principles do.

Why hope? Why not just give in to the bleakness of the yard and the discouragements of my soul? Because focusing on what is temporary, even though it may not feel like it, is always a mistake. There is something greater than the moment, an eternal reality, on which to anchor my heart. I never know this more surely than when I accompany my sister (who invites me to mention her here) to an "open meeting" for alcoholics.

Once a month the group she belongs to has a meeting to celebrate anyone who has made it through one more year of sobriety and everyone, not just alcoholics, can attend. They provide a cake and heartfelt congratulations for the miracle of another sober year. The celebrants invite a member of their group to speak at the Birthday Meeting and what they inevitably share is their battle with alcohol.

I go to these meetings occasionally because I love my sister and because, as I'm sure I've said before, it is here that I meet God's humblest saints. Oh, they might not realize that they are saints, but I can practically see God beaming through each person as they stand, say their name, and admit their addiction. Their reward? Those who understand the depths to which they have been and the battle they have fought call them by name and lovingly accept them in each "hello."

Can you imagine how powerful our churches would be if at least once a month we came in, stood in front of everyone and said "Hi, I'm Jan (or whoever you are) and I'm a sinner saved by grace." It might be even better if I had to introduce myself as addicted to terrible highway etiquette or as having terminal impatience or something specific to my character. I would love to hear the congregation respond together with gusto, "Hello, Jan!" and smile at me as if I had just baked a cake and not admitted that I am a screwball by nature made powerful and clean only by the power of a loving, amazing God. Anyway, just to keep from oversimplifying what happens in the world of AA, right after the meeting that night, one of the participants got belligerent and marched all over the serenity of several other members. I didn't say it was perfect, just amazing. I understand one of the twelve steps provides a means for those who blow it to come back later, admit their shortcomings and make amends. Those of us who meet in churches should try to keep up with the recovering alcoholic community in this as well.

Anyway, that evening the guest speaker at the event shared her story. She told us that her life had been marked from the beginning by a sense that she just didn't matter, that she was unseen and unloved. An alcoholic father, a first husband who pointed a gun with a bullet in one chamber at her head in a game of Russian Roulette shortly after their honeymoon, and eventually, a decline into hell with alcohol marked her path. Occasionally she would call the Alcoholics Anonymous "hotline" and ask what she told us was a "phony question," although she couldn't say why. I guess first steps are always tenuous. Always she denied she had any problem with drinking, while doing whatever it took to protect her addiction. Then after her second husband, also an alcoholic, tried to commit suicide she decided to go to an AA meeting. Just one meeting, she thought. At noon the following day, she told her husband what she was doing and asked if he wanted to come along. He did.

"I think they took one look at us and decided to do a First Step meeting immediately," she said with a smile. That means the AA group focused their time on the first step of recovery where you admit your life has become unmanageable because of alcohol and you are helpless to change it yourself. Giving it over to the One who can help comes in Step Three, I think, after you admit that such a power exists. Surrendering to God, the unseen Presence who is the source of all hope is the beginning of freedom for the alcoholic. As far as I've been able to tell, it is the beginning of freedom for each of us.

"I left that meeting with hope," she said. "Nothing seemed to have changed on the outside but, for the first time I had hope." Turns out that day marked the last day she's had a drink in over 14 years.

She looked intently at us as she brought her talk to a conclusion.

"I've been listening all my life to a voice saying I'm an outsider, saying that no one loves me, that I just don't belong. I heard the same voice tonight right before I came up here to share with you," she said, pausing to consider her next words. "The difference is that now I know that it is a lie. I look out on this group and I see your faces and I see the love that has helped to keep me sober all these years." Over time she learned something else about God's presence—that it is often experienced through those who love Him and who, in the process, love us, too.

She had lots more to say but the message was clear. After years of futility, she discovered hope and eventually, a full life in sobriety. She did everything to throw her life away, but in the end, she found hope instead. It began with surrender and a loving God who had the power to do for her what she could not do for herself.

For most of us, the struggle to hope is the struggle to lean into the real and away from illusion, even if it sometimes appears to be just the opposite. We lean into the Presence of a God whom we cannot see and find hope. Once we find and feed that hope it becomes the dry and fruitful land in an otherwise soggy world.

Last Saturday's get together was good for me. It reminded me that despite my occasional gloomy moods and times of doubt, despite the rain and the washed away landscape in my backyard, and despite the rain pattering on my roof this weekend, I choose hope.

As they said at the AA meeting I attended that night, "May you find it now, too."

CHAPTER 2

THE SECOND PROMISE OF HOPE: HIS PURPOSE

We hope in His Purpose.
Hope tells us that God has a purpose for us and that it is good. He is in the business of redeeming the broken and He redeems everything, both good and bad, for His children.

"And we know that God causes all things to work together for good to those who love God, to those who are called according to His purpose."

Romans 8:28 NASB

COFFINS IN THE YARD

Driving over the crest of the hill, I turned my blinker on and prepared to take a quick left into my driveway. It was a beautiful late spring evening. In Georgia that means that the air is soft and the twilight breeze drifts past you carrying the smell of honeysuckle so light and fresh and sweet that you want to bathe in it. At 8:30 in the evening there is still enough light to take a walk down the street or just sit on your front porch and watch the lingering rays of sun slowly fade, the lightning bugs blinking until the sky goes dark and the stars take over.

I barely noticed the two people pulling bags of dirt from the back of a truck across the street from my house. It hardly registered at all that there were two awkward rectangles of wood rising out of their front yard, looking a little like coffins without tops, reminiscent of something built during the civil war when they didn't have the time or tools to frame things symmetrically. These structures were clumsy and out of place lying on top of the neighbor's front lawn. As quickly as the bags of dirt were dragged off the back of the truck, they were hauled across the lawn and poured into the unsightly structures.

Oh, and did I forget to mention that these dirt filled coffin like things were lying on the front lawn right across the street from my house? It was as if someone had checked and found the exact spot where I joyfully looked out from my front window every morning and placed the objects right there, like yard pictures framed precisely by my window. Did I mention what joy and peace penetrated my heart each and every time I looked out that window? In summer, the largest cherry tree I had ever seen blossomed in that yard, draping its drooping pink flowers like a lacy shawl across the front of their house. Did I tell you that looking at this scene was a source of comfort and reassurance in the battleground of my own life? Yes, I loved that view out my front window. Yes, I did.

The reason it took me a minute to register what was going on across the street is that I was remembering what had happened during the last wonderful, unexpected hour of my life. You see, every other Tuesday night I work with a group of women at a place called Rainbow Village, where homeless women and children are given a chance to rebuild their lives. The staff there is amazing and the women who come usually stay for about a year. Their children receive after school care while the mothers learn how to find and keep a job, manage their finances, resolve conflicts, take care of themselves and live on their own.

My job was to share with them what I knew about parenting which, if you've ever been a parent, seems like a whole lot at some points in your life and very little at others. I had walked the gauntlet of parenting highs and lows, reaching what I considered the lowest point only a few years before. Things were back on track now and I had gained a compassion for other parents after my own deep struggles. So there I was, a single mother myself, sharing with women who were returning from life's edge.

One of these women and her children had been found sleeping in a storage unit that belonged to a friend. Every morning this mother used jugs of water filled at the local gas station to help get her children cleaned up and ready for school. The kids walked to the bus stop and the mother drove her only remaining asset, an older car, to work. Their biggest hope was that soon they would be sleeping in beds again. Eventually, that desire was granted when the car finally died or she lost the job. I can't remember which, but either way, someone connected her to Rainbow Village and she joined the program and began rebuilding her life. It's very humbling and, honestly, very challenging to work with those who've survived that kind of struggle. Every war takes its toll and living on the street while trying to care for your children is its own special kind of combat.

When I arrived at Rainbow Village that evening to teach, I had a lesson all prepared. Just as I was pulling the neatly packaged handouts from my bag, two participants arrived late and visibly upset. In that moment, everything changed. The lesson plans were laid aside after one woman threw a pen across the room in her anger, surprising another mother when it hit her arm. Luckily the wounded woman had the control to get up and leave the room temporarily, avoiding full scale battle. As I was trying to discover what had so upset these two women, I prayed quickly for the wisdom to know how to help.

It didn't take long for them to begin talking. In the past week, both of the women were angry had violated one or more program rules in order to take care of what they considered more important business. In other words, they had decided that something else was more critical than the Rainbow Village rules and they had acted accordingly. As a result, they were the recipients of official program warnings and some strict talking to. This served to remind them of what they considered the unfairness of life and made them once again the victims of systems they could neither control nor accommodate.

In the middle of venting their anger we began to discuss the idea that somewhere between the stimulus, or what happens to us, and the response, or how we react, we all have a moment of choice. I had learned this from Stephen Covey's *7 Habits of Highly Effective People*.[5] He'd learned it from Victor Frankl, a Jewish psychiatrist who had suffered terribly in Hitler's death camps. In his memoirs, Frankl shared his discovery that we humans can choose our response to life and to others no matter what is done to us. It's a hard truth to swallow because, after all, what about the way all those other folks are acting? Don't they deserve some blame? Doesn't their bad behavior "make me" respond poorly? Not according to Dr. Frankl.

Taking responsibility for our own actions, no matter what the circumstance, is a challenge for all of us. I've found that sometimes in the milliseconds between what someone does to me and what I do in response, the only choice I feel capable of making is to pray. This way I have some much needed help in how I choose to respond. This can be very helpful for those of us who want to make better decisions but struggle in the process.

Watching the women's' responses to this idea, I could see they wanted to argue its validity. If Frankl's suffering hadn't been at least equal to or greater than their own, they may have remained unconvinced. But it's hard to disagree with the findings of someone who was tortured in a death camp and in the process influenced his captors more than they influenced him. If he says you can choose how you respond no matter what happens to you, well, maybe you really can. The women finally agreed but not before we talked about all the times they had been the victims of injustice and all the things that were spinning out of control in their lives. One by one they began to share circumstances where they were currently reacting instead of proactively making choices. They had believed they were compelled to act as they did and ended up being prisoners of their own reactions. Now they wanted to be free to choose.

It doesn't take much imagination to picture the room at that moment, to see the mothers and the light in them as they reached out and embraced a new freedom. Watching their faces, I was reminded of all the faithful friends who prayed each week for these mothers before I came over. I silently offered a prayer of thanks that His power was present with us again. It was a wonderful moment for everyone.

So, you may ask, what does this have to do with the giant dirt boxes on the lawn across the street? I had just been to the mountain top with these mothers and I was busy surveying the beauty of the surrounding countryside. That is, until the neighbor's new view came into view. I parked my car and walked out to pick up the day's mail. It was then that it actually hit me that my new neighbors were dropping huge bags of black dirt into crooked rectangles on their front yard.

"What are you doing there?" I asked, not quite understanding yet what was going on.

"We're making a vegetable garden," the new owner said, smiling sweetly.

"Oh," I said dumbly, feeling that somehow that wasn't a good answer in a neighborhood where everyone grew their vegetables in their back yards and grass in their front.

After all, we didn't live in the country. We lived in a big city and even though we were part of a smaller community within that city, there wasn't one single other lawn within miles where this was occurring. I felt a cloud of confusion settle over my brain, like the early morning mist that blankets the local river.

"Uh, why don't you grow them in the back yard?" I finally managed to ask, shaking my head to make sense of it all.

"Not enough sun," she said, quickly filling the rectangles with more dirt and tossing the bag aside.

It wasn't until much later that I came up with the helpful thought that her problem was easily remedied with the application of a saw to a few tree branches out back. For the moment, an uneasy feeling settled over me and I headed back to my house, looking blankly at each piece of mail. By the time I reached the garage door it occurred to me that putting that much dirt into a structure on the front yard wasn't designed to be temporary.

I walked back out, still not sure what was wrong with this situation and asked my new neighbors one more question. "You aren't going to leave those there, are you?" I asked, pointing to the clumsy structures.

After a quite innocent looking nod of their heads, they affirmed that they were indeed planning to leave the crooked piles in the front yard, on top of the grass, in the middle of my beautiful view. I headed back to my house yet again. Once inside, another question occurred to me.

Once more I headed back to the curb, trying not to look like an interfering neighbor while feeling like a little interference was exactly what was called for here.

"By the way," I said innocently in the growing darkness, "have you checked with the city to see if they have a rule against this? They have a whole squad of folks who come by regularly, driving through the neighborhood and inspecting our houses just to make sure we're all following the city codes. Code enforcement is what they are all about and they can really be obnoxious," I went on, hoping in my heart that they would be obnoxious enough to stop this view ruining effort of my new neighbors.

"We'll check with them in the morning," they replied and ignoring me, returned to shoveling dirt.

I trudged back to my house and went inside, sitting down heavily in the big blue chair in my den. I began reviewing in my mind the litany of wrongs being committed across the street. Who would put things like that in their front yard? Haven't these people looked around and noticed that no-one else, and I mean no one, is growing veggies up front? Especially not in raised beds surrounded by unpainted 4 by 4s. They looked so much like coffins that later another neighbor suggested we go to a party store and get a skeleton hand to droop over the edge of the bed, showing the creepy structures up for what they really were—the work of the undead.

Another thought occurred to me. "You can choose, you know. You can choose how to respond to this. In between the stimulus of dirt filled, crooked coffins and your reaction, which is starting to heat up, you can choose another way to look at this!"

I thought about how I challenged the women at Rainbow Village to look at matters of life and survival through the eyes of choice, deciding that they didn't have to be victims no matter what others had done or were doing to them. I knew it was ridiculous to be so upset about my ruined view. It may be hard for you to understand why this was so important to me. Over the past few years I had become a sponge for anything that gave me a sense of peace. Of course, I'm sure that was true of the Rainbow Village mothers as well.

Now let me just share with you that this happens to me a lot. As soon as I open my big mouth to help someone else learn something new, darned if those words don't come back to haunt me. I find myself challenged to live out the truths I share with others and I have to tell you, sometimes it's downright annoying when it happens. I'd just finished teaching, it had been a long day, I was helping others, and my reward? Dirt shoveling neighbors with civil war structures filling my once peaceful view.

Nevertheless, I wasn't ready to let go yet. I gave a cursory nod to the idea that I could control my reaction and be proactive. Then I closed the blinds in the front windows.

A few days later I came home to find three bales of hay with tomato plants spouting from the top of each one in my neighbor's front yard. Until that moment I had thought you just grew tomatoes out of the ground like all the other veggies. Was it really necessary to put them in bales of hay next to the coffins on the front yard? The principle of "you can choose" was beginning to experience some serious difficulty in my thoughts.

The very next morning I called the Code Enforcement folks, who in the past had insisted I take down my tasteful tiny twinkling lights from around my porch because they were out of code. It didn't seem to matter to them that the city itself had lights just like mine that decorated the trees on the main street in town. I asked them about the hay bales and coffins.

"No rules against raised beds or vegetable gardens in the front yard," the woman on the phone said calmly. I had learned since my initial encounter with my neighbors that they were planning to put up a fence in front of the coffins to, according to them, help improve the view. For some reason this didn't reassure me at all. Maybe because, again, there were no fences in front yards in our neighborhood. That's right, not a single one. We all fenced up our back yards where we grew our robust blooming vegetables and harvested the goods.

"What about fences in the front yard?" I whined. "Surely there is some code about those?"

"Nope," the woman said. "No one else in the city has a fence in their front yard, or a vegetable garden, so we haven't bothered with a code about either. You could send us a request and we could put it before the city board."

"How long would that take?" I asked.

"Oh, it'll be next month before they meet," she replied sweetly.

I could feel the impending sense of doom fall over me. It was no good. I was up against a pro. The code enforcement folks had no qualms about what was happening. Just because they had taken down my twinkling lights, didn't mean piles of dirt in rickety structures along with hay bales right next to the street would take away from our community's view.

Adding insult to injury was the fact that I had spent a fair amount of time praying about getting just the right people to buy that house across the street. It had twice been owned by very strange people, one of whom could be found knocking down her mailbox at midnight while ignoring an entire herd of unspayed cats living in her garage. The owners before her had invited ancient spirit guides to join them on a daily basis and told us about it whenever they had the chance. Don't get me wrong, I liked these neighbors fine but you have to admit their activities were a little unusual. When the house had gone up for sale again, I thought maybe it was time to take preventive measures. So every day for several months I had prayed, "Lord, please bring just the right person to buy the house across the street."

Now the answer to my prayers had created a little rift between God and me.

"Lord," I complained, "I prayed for months about the right individual buying that house. I asked you to send a responsible person to live across from me. In the past I've had a series of crazy and confused people staring at me from over there but as long as they didn't mess with the view I was fine. I was so sure that you had answered my prayer! What happened?"

A thought passed through my mind. "I did answer the prayer. Are you going to trust Me?"

I wasn't sure. Why should I? Why couldn't God just answer my prayers the way I wanted them answered? Had he misunderstood what I meant by "just the right person?" Didn't he want me to look out my window and feel peaceful? This prayer thing can be more complicated than it seems.

Now I was faced with the double "choosing" whammy. Not only was I responsible to choose my response to this unsettling situation, but I was also feeling compelled to choose to trust God, whom I know listens to all my prayers. After a fair amount of struggling I finally realized that in the big scheme of life's important issues this one didn't rate very high. I decided to "choose" to trust God. That meant that every day, as the devastation in the front yard across the street continued, I chose to pray for my new neighbor. You'll have to trust me that those prayers had nothing to do with the yard and everything to do with blessing the owner of the yard.

Some interesting things began to happen that had nothing to do with the lawn, or should I say the missing lawn? It turned out the house across the street had not been taken care of over the years. As the new owner, who had not moved in yet but only left hay bales in the front yard, hired some contractors to make fixes, she uncovered more than she expected. When replacing the kitchen floor she found mold. The next thing you know all the flooring had been pulled up and the mold people descended upon the house. Luckily, they were able to get rid of it. Then the entire kitchen was rebuilt. My new neighbor's cousins came in from North Dakota to take over a rather prolonged period of repairing and rebuilding the house. It took about eight months before all that was wrong with the place was fixed. It only took me a short time to start feeling a little sorry for this person who bought a house that needed so much mending.

My new neighbor's mother, father and brother also joined in the repairing. She apparently had the full support of her family to make her house almost completely new on the inside. At one point I met the cousins and gave them a little welcoming basket I had put together for the owner. I shared some of the veggies from my own backyard with the mother. The brother was a kind, likeable, no nonsense guy who was happy to keep an eye out for unwelcome intruders after we had a robbery in the neighborhood. All the while, the grass died out in the front yard across the street and eventually corn was planted in front of the short "fence" that had popped up out there. That one really got me. Why put a fence up to hide the coffin garden and then plant corn in front of it? It isn't really considered a decorative plant, is it?

Finally, almost a year after she purchased the house, the new resident moved in. Think about that—a whole year fixing, repairing and making whole a house that you purchased to live in. I could only hope she didn't pay full price for it. The structure of the house had been in jeopardy and this woman had a family who was willing to help her make some important changes for its long term good.

I've decided that maybe God just looks at things differently than I do. I'm thinking it's possible that He did indeed answer my original prayers and found a buyer who would lovingly restore the house across the street, even if I didn't approve of her front yard strategy. After all, isn't He more concerned with what's on the inside than on the outside in general?

The concept of choosing to trust God and choosing my reaction to what happens has been a challenge for me but one that I've learned to appreciate. Somewhere during the "year of the grassless yard" I was reminded that if you can't trust God when things don't look good, well, why bother trusting Him at all? Didn't He tell us in His word that "all things work together for good for those who love God?" I had hoped for one thing and gotten another. But in the end, wasn't it better to have someone invest in saving the house itself than to continue to have an uninterrupted view of a cute yard and lovely tree?

It's spring now and the somewhat raggedy garden across the street is slowly coming back to life. In my yard the grass has welcomed an unusual amount of clover and moss after a very wet winter so who am I to complain about hay bales and an unpainted fence? When I looked out the window this morning, the tree was beginning to bloom and it was lovely enough to distract me from the old wicker chair leaning crookedly behind the fence near the empty plastic containers lying on their sides.

Every day, I am still choosing to pray for my neighbor. Is it possible that this was the real purpose of all this? That the only way I would be so consistent in asking God to bless this person was if He challenged me to trust Him in the face of something I didn't want?

Still, nobody is perfect. Turns out I spend more time in my back yard nowadays where I can I feel the breeze as it blows through the leaves of the old trees, causing them to sway back and forth in a timeless dance. The good news is that I have finally stopped worrying about the yard across the street. Not that I'd mind a little grass, but it turns out that all that praying has had an interesting effect. It has given me time to get to know my neighbor and start to enjoy her and her family for who they are. Recently they kindly offered me an offshoot of the giant cherry tree that had seeded in their yard. It is now planted next to my mailbox and I'm dreaming of the day when it blossoms its magnificent lacy curtain in my own yard.

I think I'm finally starting to get it. Sometimes it just takes me a little time to catch on. Now that I've had the opportunity to practice trusting God and choosing to be proactive, I've decided to put these new skills to work in another area of my life. I've started praying that someday our city's Code Enforcement will allow me to put my twinkling lights back up on the front porch.

I can't wait to see how God answers this one.

THE GIFTS

It was Christmas time. It was busy. I was distracted. What can I say? I had no idea when friends and family would be at home, or off making eggnog with the neighbors, or at Home Depot picking out a tree. Because I was already out on errands myself that day, I didn't bother to check before I drove the extra fifteen minutes north, hoping to catch Debbie, a close friend of mine, at home.

In my possession I had a reasonably unique Christmas present, lovingly picked out just for her. When I am in the mountains of north Georgia or the Carolinas, I am consistently drawn to the products of local artisans; hand laced brooms in brilliant colors, hand blown glass pendants that hang fashionably on your necklace, or plants potted in old pieces of wood. This year I had found several items that seemed special. One was a "soap rock" scented with lavender that looked just like a gemstone carved from the side of a cave. I'd also found a business card holder blown from brightly colored glass into a lovely oval shape. Unable to decide which one I wanted to give Debbie, I decided to buy both of them for her.

As I pulled into her driveway, I knew right away that my timing was off. The house and garage were empty. Disappointed but in a hurry, I left her gift on the back doorstep and returned to my car. It was a bit of a letdown. In my mind's eye I had been picturing Debbie opening her gifts, smiling as she caught the scent of the soap and then again as she placed one of her tiny badges of identity in the card holder's swirling glass enclosure. I resigned myself to waiting until the following week to discover whether I'd chosen well for her this year.

The days passed and so did the holiday. A quick call to wish my friend and her family a Merry Christmas was all the time we had to share. With last minute shopping, family gatherings and the exhaustion that follows all the yuletide activity, we were lost in our respective worlds. About a week later I thought of Debbie again and my curiosity got the best of me. I wanted to know what she thought of her presents. Touching her number under "favorites" on my cell phone, I called and was glad to find her at home.

After some small talk I finally asked her, "How did you like your Christmas presents?"

She gushed. "They are wonderful! I've put the soap in my upstairs bath and it looks and smells wonderful. I really love that scent and it is so beautiful! There is one small problem though." She hesitated for a second, confused.

"What's that?" I asked.

"Well," Debbie said, sounding a little puzzled, "The soap doesn't quite fit in the holder. I placed it on top anyway, but it looks like it's ready to fall off any minute."

"What?" I asked again. I paused and tried to put the pieces together in my mind. I thought about the two gifts I had given her and wondered what they had to do with each other.

After a moment I asked her, "Why are you trying to put your soap rock in a business card holder?"

We hesitated for a split second and then simultaneously burst into laughter. I was picturing the soap, its lovely fragrance filling the bathroom, balanced precariously on the edge of something designed to live on a desk and dispense business cards. Without any input from me, Debbie had automatically assumed that the two presents belonged together. She was determined to make sure they worked in harmony, even if that meant a shaky alliance on the counter.

I'm betting that Debbie isn't the only one who has tried to use a gift for something it wasn't designed to do. Without hearing from the giver of a present it might be simpler than we think to make assumptions that don't always translate into reality. What if putting soap into card holders is more the rule than the exception in life? What if we presume to understand the moments of our existence but, not having asked life's Giver and Designer, we are only seeing a partial picture?

It was easy for my friend to suppose that the items I gave her were complimentary. She could have spent years trying to make the combination work together. If she washed her hands enough, she might have eventually gotten the soap to fit in the container. But it simply wasn't designed to go there. Both items had unique uses that apparently required a simple explanation from the giver before they could be properly operated.

People aren't the only ones who can get confused in this arena. Sarah the bloodhound is a good example of how this plays out in the animal kingdom. Sarah was one of two rescue dogs featured in a recent television special. She was a plain dog, big and lanky with long droopy ears and a sad-sack face. Left at an animal shelter by a previous owner, she was currently living in a foster home. As I watched Sarah tearing up her temporary owner's home, the show's announcer explained that when bored she would chew on her chains, munch on the couch or pillows and in general, destroy whatever she could find. She lived in a small environment with little to do so she occupied her time eating her surroundings. Sarah's well-meaning adoptive parents wanted to help her but, surrounded by a cloud of cushion filling, they were at their wits end.

Then, Vern came on the scene. From years of experience training bloodhounds, he immediately understood that Sarah was misusing her special gifts. He knew that she was designed to do something specific and because he knew that, he was hopeful that he could help her.

As he began working with Sarah, Vern discovered that she was afraid of loud noises and uninterested in the smell of blood. Bloodhounds are born with an innate talent for finding things by following a sensory trail but Sarah didn't appear to catch on. While this was problematic, Vern wasn't discouraged. He had a reason to hope. He knew Sarah's gifts and purpose. He knew what she was designed to do.

He began to train Sarah to recognize a scent and track it down. While he was at it, Vern also helped the dog overcome her fear of sudden noises. Like many of us, Sarah had experiences from her past that were barriers to her future. Not only did she need to learn how to use her natural gifts, she needed emotional healing in the process. Eventually, as she experienced that healing, the pull of doing what she was designed to do was so powerful, and Vern was so patient and persistent, that Sarah became an expert tracker. No more chain eating for her! Once she discovered her talents and felt the excitement of exercising them, why would she return to chains?

I think I've done the same kind of thing as Sarah the bloodhound. When bored or without direction, I have occasionally been known to create disorder and confusion in my own surroundings. I've acted as if I am made to get the most I can from life, but aren't I really designed to give? I've misinterpreted my freedom to choose with the thought that my Designer doesn't need to be involved with my choices. I've ignored my own internal makeup and tried to be like others rather than becoming more of what I was designed for. It's easier to get confused than you might think.

I guess that means I don't always ask the Giver before I use the gift. I have to tell you that it's not a strategy that has worked well for me and I've certainly tried it at least as much as Sarah. If you've ever felt like eating the furniture, or even just throwing it or jumping on it in frustration, then you may have been experiencing the same sense of confusion that Sarah, my friend Debbie and I have all felt. You might just need some help to understand the purpose of your gifts.

As for me, I have been learning some things along the way about how I'm put together. According to the Good Book, I am not randomly formed. I have been knit together in my mother's womb and God has counted every hair on my head. Plus, I have a purpose and it can only be found when I ask the Gift Giver to make things clear for me. As I have begun to think about all this, it has led to a kind of hope that isn't shaken when things go badly. If there is a purpose in the design and a design in the purpose, I can demonstrate resiliency in the face of uncertainty. Maybe I can even think of how to use my gifts to help myself and others around me to move on to the next good thing in life.

As for Debbie, I'm happy that before the soap melted away into the card holder I had a chance to show her the best use for her presents. It wasn't any time at all before she began washing and placing the soap lovingly in a real soap dish. Meanwhile, she whisked her business card holder off to work and left it on her desk. Her name and contact information are now fashionably displayed in her office and readily available to those who need it.

It may have taken a little explanation to get everything right but it was worth it. Now that she knows, Debbie has high hopes that her

Christmas gifts, each with its own special purpose, will serve her well. It's possible that they will even do a little more than the obvious. Maybe, just maybe, they will help connect her with the people who are purposefully strewn in her path.

NO EYE HAS SEEN, NO EAR HAS HEARD

"I was so young when it all happened," she said and then took a bite of her salad. Her eyes wandered off as if she were reaching back into that time and place, peering over the edge of some memory long ago put to rest. She smiled slightly at me and continued with her story.

Susan had already shared that she was the product of a church going family and had married young, straight out of college, with a world of opportunity before her. Her life was as close to perfect as you could get. Both she and her husband had good jobs and it wasn't long before they had their first child; a healthy, happy and compliant baby boy.

"Keith was the perfect child. From the very beginning he was no trouble at all. We never had a problem with him. A few years later I got pregnant again. We were living the life."

She paused to take a sip of water before she continued. Susan was wearing a tailored business suit with just the tiniest bit of flair in its waistline. Her medium length brown hair flipped at her shoulders and gave the impression that she was still a college student. She is actually a very savvy business woman, a partner for her clients, helping each one to build their business with her expertise. I'd just learned that she had won an award at work for selling more than any of her peers by more than double. She blushed when I mentioned it.

"You weren't supposed to know about that," she said as she glanced down at her plate, a little embarrassed by my praise.

There is something so genuine about Susan. When I told her I was writing a book about hope and that I wanted to include some other people's true stories, she had piped up, "I have a lot of those. "

"You do?" I asked, a little surprised by her quick response.

"Oh, yes!" Her smile widened and she nodded her head. "A lot of them."

I was intrigued and asked if she would be willing to share some of her life. She agreed and that is how we ended up having lunch that Wednesday in the small cafeteria at my company's headquarters. We didn't have much time before my next meeting and Susan was just getting started. I urged her to continue her story so I wouldn't have to stop her in the middle to make my next deadline.

"Go ahead," I said.

"I was eight months pregnant with my second child when my sister came from Atlanta to visit me. We were living in Dallas, Texas at the time," she said.

When her sister arrived, she took one look at Susan and said, "Wow! You don't look very pregnant!"

It hadn't occurred to Susan that she was small or that her sister's observation was the first indication of something gone terribly wrong for her and her family. By the end of that same week Susan's belly had gotten so large, she couldn't bend down to tie her shoes. At her doctor's appointment the next week she learned why.

She was shocked to learn that her seemingly ordinary pregnancy was anything but. Her baby had a genetic condition called Trisomy 18. This meant there was a problem with the Trisomy 18 gene and her baby was missing two chambers of his heart and his stomach. There was no hope that he could survive, no children born with that condition had ever lived longer than 30 days. The reason Susan had gotten so large in such a short time was that the amniotic fluid was building up because the baby had stopped processing it.

"The baby cannot survive with this condition," the doctor told her.

He went on to say that she needed to decide whether she wanted to terminate the pregnancy at that point. If she didn't and the child was born, the hospital and doctors would have to do everything possible to prolong his life. The cost could potentially use up their lifetime limit of insurance and even so, the baby would not survive. If she waited, she would only prolong the inevitable at great risk to herself and her family.

Over the next week Susan went through a battery of tests while she and her husband spoke with their minister, doctors and a genetic counselor. They prayed and they talked and they prayed some more. A team of doctors at the hospital reviewed all the facts of her case. And all the while Susan felt as if she was in a suspended reality.

"I was paralyzed," she told me. "Time would just go by and I wouldn't be aware of it. I remember leaning down to tie my shoes and when I looked up, two hours had passed. When I looked down again, I could see that my shoes still weren't tied."

At the end of that week, Susan, at 26 years of age, made a decision that racked her heart to its core. She and her husband felt the only thing to do was to terminate the pregnancy.

"I didn't have the emotional or spiritual fortitude to wait out the final month," she told me later. She had been told that her child could not survive and that it was a matter of facing that fact in the present or near future.

I tried to imagine how hard this all must have been on her and I felt my heart wrench at the thought of what she had been through. She was carrying a child both she and her husband wanted to have. She had lived with the tiny being inside of her for eight months only to find out that this baby was unable to survive no matter what choice she made for it. I pictured her unable to think or even move, with every hour ticking by almost unnoticed. All the while, this young woman was frozen with the weight of needing to decide what she should do until the heaviness of having made that decision took its place.

It took a week to reach the final conclusion but only a day to put things into motion. After twelve hours of labor, her second child arrived, no longer alive, weighing three and a half pounds. Susan and her husband and her mother held him and grieved for this baby who would never be a part of their tiny family. Then, they had a funeral for their second child. Her mother, who had always been close to Susan, went home to her job and Susan and her husband tried to move forward.

A week after the baby's birth and death was Mother's Day. Susan and her tiny family decided to spend that weekend doing something that

fed their hearts and gave them time together to recover—they would go camping.

"I know it seems strange," she told me, "but I was young and in good shape. Physically I was ok, even though I was spent emotionally. I knew my family was hurting too. Keith, my 5 year old, had a stuffed duck that he had wrapped in a blanket and was carrying around with him. He had been waiting for a baby brother to come home from the hospital and one never arrived. I wanted a chance to spend time with him and reassure him. I wanted to be with my husband, a chance to feel some peace, to get away and clear my head. At that point, I was planning to go back to work the following Monday."

The campground they chose was in Oklahoma, a place called Broken Bow State Park. Unlike much of the rest of the state, the park was filled with hills and trees and lakes, providing an unexpected refuge for their family. They stayed at their campsite Saturday night and got up Sunday, planning on going canoeing. Unfortunately the place that rented the canoes did not open until one in the afternoon so they decided to go horseback riding instead.

"That must sound odd," Susan said to me, maybe noticing the surprise on my face.

I had ridden horses for years and I had also had two children. I couldn't imagine riding a week after delivering a baby but she was undaunted.

"The baby was so small I had less to recover from than normal," she commented. "I had always loved to ride and was good at it."

So she, her husband, her little boy and their guide saddled up and headed off on horseback that Mother's Day morning. About an hour into the ride, a storm began to gather. They were on a hilly trail surrounded by trees when suddenly Susan's horse went berserk. When I asked her what happened, she said she didn't know if it was actually the smell or sounds of the impending storm or if the horse had seen a snake. Whatever it was, the animal took off through the heavily wooded area at full speed, out of control.

"The horse would stop only long enough to rear up and then he would take off again," Susan said. "I knew he was crazy and I began to pray, 'Lord, please don't let this horse fall. Please, don't let him fall on me.' It was terrifying."

She felt sure that if the huge animal fell on her it would kill her. She could feel the tree limbs hitting her face as they raced through the forest. Unable to think of a way to get off without hitting a tree, she held on for dear life. Finally they came into a very small clearing. Suddenly her mount raised its front hoofs into the air one last time and she was flung from its back to the ground.

"I became aware that I was in the dirt and my left arm was lying at an odd angle to my body. My right leg wouldn't move. I was dazed. At that moment, it began to rain," Susan said.

Lying on that spot in the middle of a hilly Oklahoma park, Susan, her husband and her child waited for the rescue crew to come for her.

"I am in hell. Am I being punished for what I did?" she thought as she lay there waiting for help to arrive. It was all she could think as the time ticked by.

"That is when I started to really shut down," she told me. "I had just gone through the worst thing in my life a week before and now this. It was too overwhelming. I began to feel numb."

It took several hours to get the stretcher into the woods and carry her back out to the ambulance.

"It turns out I had a compound fracture in my arm. My leg had what the doctor called a 'jammed break,' not unlike the victim of a car crash whose leg gets jammed into the dashboard. I had never had a broken bone in my life," Susan said.

She continued, "The first hospital we went to was tiny and was basically unable to help. They cleaned me up, gave me some pain medicine, put a splint on my arm and sent me to a larger hospital nearby. There my leg was x-rayed and I was told that I would need surgery to put pins in my leg. That was when we decided to head back home to Dallas."

It was nighttime by then and her husband put Susan in the back seat of their car and their young son up front with him. As they drove through the Oklahoma night, the sky began to change and a storm came in. On the radio they listened intently to the news that there were tornadoes springing up in their area. They continued driving, right through the gray skies and high winds, with tornadoes threatening on every side and Susan lying frozen in the back seat of the car.

"My husband kept saying over and over, "I'm so sorry. I should never have let this happen. I'm going to get you home," she told me. They drove through the night until they finally reached Dallas early the next morning.

The neighbors saw them arrive and came over. They helped to carry her from the car to the house and put her in bed. Once she was settled in, she had one more thing to do. Susan called her mother to tell her what had happened. Not only was it Mother's Day, it was also her mother's birthday.

Immediately her mom offered to return and help take care of her but Susan refused. Her mother had just spent the previous week with them and was present at her baby's birth and funeral. She told her not to come back and reassured her that she would be fine.

Within three days Susan was back at work. She went to a specialist the day they returned to Dallas who suggested she not have surgery and pins as they might cause problems for her later in life. Instead he suggested she get casted and stay in a wheelchair for three months. Her leg would be unable to bear any weight during that time but she would be better off in the long run. So that is what she did.

"How did you go back to work so soon?" I asked, amazed at the thought that you could lose a child, break several bones, drive through a tornado and go back to work all within a week or so. "How in the world did you get to work every day?"

"The city had public transportation called DART and something called HandyRide for the disabled," she explained. "Every day a taxi would pick me up. Riding with me in the taxi were three other people--a woman who was blind, another woman going to cancer treatment, and a mentally handicapped young man. Looking at the permanent disability of some of these other people was one of the things that helped me keep perspective about what had happened to me."

During this time, several things were happening in Susan's heart. The thought that she was being punished continued to haunt her. She was determined to show that she could work through it all, maybe hoping she could somehow redeem herself with an effort of her will. Nevertheless, every day she realized how deeply dependent she was on others. Her husband took care of both her and her son while he continued to go to work. Every morning he bathed her, washed and dried her hair, dressed her and put her in the taxi with her wheelchair. Once she arrived at work, the security guard came out of the building, got her out of the car, put her into her wheelchair, and pushed her into the building. Neighbors, coworkers and people from their local church cooked for them every day. Susan told me she didn't have to cook a single meal for those three months. She was overwhelmed with the kindness of others and slowly her heart began to change.

Susan explained to me that she had always been a churchgoer but she had never really applied her faith. During this time, she turned more and more to her Bible, seeking to understand what had happened and what she should do. She became more convinced that her power came not from proving what she could do, not by doing it all herself, but rather by letting go so that God could provide the strength she needed.

"Before all this happened I thought that because I worked hard, when good things happened to me, I deserved them. During this period I was becoming a different person. I recognized that the people in that taxi with me every day had been dealt a hand they didn't cause or deserve. Life wasn't as simple as I had assumed. I had taken a lot for granted and now I was becoming more compassionate."

Susan was discovering that sometimes things happened for another reason and her view point on life was changing.

One day, as she was reading her Bible, she came across a scripture that overcame her. It was 1 Corinthians 2:9. *"No eye has seen, no ear has heard, and no mind has imagined what God has prepared for those who love him."*

"A thought came into my mind when I read that," Susan said. "I thought, 'If this many bad things can happen to one person, surely this many good things could happen too.' I got the feeling that things weren't going to continue the way they had been going. I began to think that God had a plan for my life. I began to have hope."

This happened about six weeks into her recovery and planted a seed that was to grow and take Susan through one last unexpected event in her life. For the next nine months she continued to mature in her faith. She could not get rid of the thought that even though many bad things had happened to her, just as many good things could happen as well.

"On April 30th, exactly one year after my baby's birth and burial, I woke up to a phone call from my aunt. My mother, who was active in her church, had gone hiking and rappelling off a local mountain near her home in Nashville, Tennessee. She was in her sixties but she was very active," Susan revealed.

Her aunt gave her some news that devastated her. "Your mother has died," she said. "She fell off the cliff where she was rappelling with her church group." Susan choked, barely able to get the words out.

"Oddly enough," Susan told me, "the place where my mother fell off the mountain was called Heaven's Door."

Susan continued. "It was one year to the day since I had lost my baby and I was overwhelmed to learn of my mother's death. My brother, sister and I got together and went up to the funeral."

Susan said that despite how hard it was, she realized that she couldn't have dealt with her mother's death the same way a year before. Something had happened in her heart during the intervening months that had given Susan an unexpected spiritual reserve. Together with her sister and brother, Susan went to clean out her mother's townhouse before they had to return home.

This is the point in Susan's story where the last piece fell into place. I can still see her as she sat across from me and told me the final part of her tale. Her words brought what she experienced to life so clearly it was as if I could see the scene unfold before me.

"When we went into my mother's house it was clear she hadn't expected to be away for long. Little things were left lying around as if she would be back to use them at any minute. I kept thinking she didn't know that she was putting each item down for the last time before she left that weekend. She hadn't prepared for someone to walk into her life like this. As I looked around I could see her life take shape before me. There were Bible verses everywhere—on the refrigerator, the bathroom mirror, all over the house. She was rebuilding her life after the death of our dad a few years before."

Susan looked thoughtful, reviewing the scene in her mind. "I kept thinking, what would someone think of me if they walked into my life this way? Would they be inspired? Motivated? What I saw in front of me was the reflection of a peaceful, spiritual life."

On her mother's bedside table was a Bible and next to the bible was one more scripture. Written on a small piece of paper, sitting next to her mother's bed, Susan read the words that had come to mean so much to her over the past year. "No eye has seen, no ear has heard, no mind has imagined what God has prepared for those who love him." Susan picked up the piece of paper. She still has it. The verse that had spoken to her during her greatest challenge had been given to her one more time—this time from her mother. Something inside her shifted and those words of hope were sealed in her heart.

It was the last part of her transformation. A year before, Susan had lived her life convinced that she was self- sufficient and in control. Even in the midst of her tragedies she wanted to prove she could make it on her own. But something in her had broken and she had found a new freedom. She realized she couldn't do it all herself and didn't need to. She began asking God to do for her what she couldn't do for herself. The way she saw others changed as well and the knowledge that there was a plan, no matter the circumstances, took root in her.

"Every time I hear that verse of scripture and think about how we've no idea what God has prepared for us, the thought comes to me that God has a plan for my life, that good is coming and that the plan still exists even when bad things happen," she shared with me as she prepared to leave that day.

As Susan would say, as many bad things have happened to you, that many good things can happen as well. Whatever it looks like now, God has a plan for you. And nothing, not grief or brokenness or even the loss of loved ones, can stop what He is doing in and for you.

Chapter 3

THE THIRD PROMISE OF HOPE: HIS PROVISION

We hope in His Provision.
Hope tells us God will provide "our daily bread," that He will take us to the next step in our journey.

"Don't worry about anything; instead, pray about everything. Tell God what you need, and thank him for all he has done."

Philippians 4:6 NLT

LIVING BETWEEN THE PROMISE AND THE COMMAND

It was the second time around that got to me. I was four weeks into recovering from the first time and had felt sure there wouldn't be a recurrence. Then, in that instant when I realized that I wasn't imagining it, fear crept over me. The fear stunned my brain like a jellyfish encounter—both stinging and paralyzing my thoughts at the same time. I got up from the chair in hopes of walking it off, like when I was young and hurt myself playing ball. I remember my coach yelling enthusiastically, "Shake it off!" when I'd get hurt during a game. So, off I'd go, hobbling around on my broken parts or waving them in the air, hoping that the act of using them again would somehow make them well. Sometimes it worked, sometimes it didn't. In this particular instance, it didn't.

However, this wasn't a ballgame. This was my life and I was experiencing vertigo for the second time in a month. Vertigo, or Benign Positional Vertigo as it's known in medical circles, is often the result of a little known function of the inner ear that has gone terribly wrong. You see, we have these tiny microscopic crystals locked in our inner ear and if we get a virus or somehow disturb them, they can move. Unfortunately they move into one of three canals where they don't belong and they cause all sorts of trouble. It's sort of a like an oil spill. If the oil escapes from its place of origin into the water, the results are a big mess with everything malfunctioning and covered in destructive goo. With vertigo, once the crystals escape their true home in your inner ear and wander into one of your canals, you wake up to find the world is spinning.

I've talked to lots of folks about this since it happened to me and, in my completely unscientific and informal survey, maybe 10% of the people I spoke to have experienced it themselves. No one smiles when you mention it. A few weeks ago I was speaking at a career networking event and asked those who'd experienced vertigo what it felt like.

"Like you are leaning to one side and always off balance," one of them said.

"You run into walls," said another.

"Like you want to throw up," said the third.

I'll stick with those descriptions for now. Suffice it to say the world spins and unless you really enjoy watching the world roll over and over in front of you, it's not fun.

With the return of my vertigo, I was scared. I'd spent a month in what I thought was a healing phase and now the dang thing had come back. The fear that fell over me was as real as if I'd been living in a paranormal movie. There was no place to go to escape. I called my sister and she agreed to come over and keep me sane and safe. Then I decided to check in with God. After a few minutes of prayer, which consisted mostly of me saying over and over again, 'Help, Lord!' I decided to check my emails at work. That may sound crazy on several levels. How can you read an email if you are spinning? Why would you want to look at your email from work on a Sunday afternoon when you aren't feeling well? I don't know what I was thinking at that moment, but for some reason it seemed like a good idea. So, I logged on to my computer and started reading.

Somewhere around the third message, I found an email from a friend who was about to lose his second job in a year. His current temporary assignment had run out. In his angst, he'd sent me this note:

"Jan, I'm finishing up my last week with my company and I'm feeling a little off. It makes me think of my favorite Psalm."

This was interesting—a work email with a Psalm in it. It certainly got my attention. He went on to quote a part of Psalm 107. Here is what it said:

- *²³ Others went out on the sea in ships;*
  they were merchants on the mighty waters.

- *²⁴ They saw the works of the LORD,*
  his wonderful deeds in the deep.

- *²⁵ For he spoke and stirred up a tempest*
  that lifted high the waves.

- *²⁶ They mounted up to the heavens and went down to the*
  depths; in their peril their courage melted away.

- *²⁷ They reeled and staggered like drunken men;*
  they were at their wits' end.

- *²⁸ Then they cried out to the LORD in their trouble,*
  and he brought them out of their distress.

- *²⁹ He stilled the storm to a whisper;*
  the waves of the sea were hushed.

- *³⁰ They were glad when it grew calm,*
  and he guided them to their desired haven.
  Psalm 107:23-30 NIV

OK, call me crazy but I didn't realize there was a description of vertigo in the Bible. I mean, it was as if the author of this psalm had gone through exactly what I was experiencing. Things were going up and down, people were reeling and staggering like they were drunk and everyone was at their wits end. I could certainly relate.

As my pastor Andy Stanley says, "You should read the Bible. You won't believe what's in there."

At that moment I couldn't have agreed with him more. The message of the psalm was completely unexpected although much appreciated. Then, when I'd finished reading it, something surprising happened to me. My fear just evaporated. It was like a rock had been lifted off my heart and I could breathe again. I was still spinning, my life continued to feel out of control, and I still didn't know how I'd make it to work the next day. But I wasn't afraid anymore. I realized something powerful at that moment. There is a huge difference between facing hard times with fear and facing them without fear. An assurance came over me and I thought, "God knows what is happening and He is with me." My fear vanished in response to the Psalm, disappearing as quickly as it had come.

That absolute peace stayed with me for about five days. The vertigo stayed too. As things continued to look uncertain and I continued spinning, the fear began to slowly creep back. I went to a new Ear, Nose and Throat specialist who did all kinds of tests. He declared my crystals had moved into Canal Two on Inner Ear Row but confidently told me he could move them back. He was unsuccessful the first time he tried and the whispers of fear were a little louder. They weren't devastating; they were more like shadows following me quietly around, creating unwanted dark corners at every turn. The doctor finally stopped the spinning on the second visit and told me it could take anywhere from three weeks to three months before the residual dizziness went away.

At this point I began to feel hopeful again but this time my lack of fear was centered in my circumstances, my lack of whirling, as well as in the message from the Psalm. I had received what appeared to be a promise from God—that He would calm my storm—and now I was experiencing some relief from my situation. It was a week before Christmas and I was taking ten days off over the holidays which should help give me time to finish healing. I hoped that I would begin my new year as good as new.

During this time my children came into town from opposite ends of the country, Nebraska and Florida, and I spent my energy enjoying them and our extended family. We celebrated the birth of Jesus and all that happened to our world as a result. We took my mom to the art museum. We visited a new church when ours was full on Christmas Eve. We had dinner with family and together we opened presents with great enthusiasm. All was well in the world.

Two days after Christmas, we had another event to celebrate—my birthday. On morning of my big day, I got up early and tiptoed around, letting the kids catch up on their sleep after all the Christmas festivities. Pouring a cup of hot tea, I sat down to think about my year.

At that moment, in the quiet and peace of my house, with my children only a dream's breath away, a surge of dizziness unexpectedly came over me. It felt like an ocean wave, tipping me off balance and threatening to sweep me over. Right behind the dizziness came another wave—a wave of fear. When I had first read the Psalm and realized God was aware of and present in my situation, my fear had immediately disappeared. Then, over the past few weeks as the dizziness stayed with me, the fear began to nibble at the edges of my thoughts. I had assumed if I could hold on, I would recover. The delay was confusing but I kept repeating the lines from the Psalm about God stilling the storm, hushing the waves, and leading the sailors to their desired haven.

I had pictured myself like one of those sailors, arriving in that haven—a world free of dizziness and full of renewed energy. I believed He had given me a promise and He would still my storm and hush my waves. No matter how I looked at it, I couldn't bring myself to believe the second onset of vertigo and my almost immediate reading of that particular Psalm, sent to my email at work at that particular time, was a coincidence. But now the vertigo had come back and the promise of the Psalm felt less sure.

"What will I do if this continues?" I thought. "How can I keep working? Being dizzy has taken all my energy even while I'm on vacation. What will happen when the demands of work and the new-year catch up with me next week? I don't think I can do this much longer."

As a single parent with two children, I had faced many challenges through the years. With God's help we had always made it through our tough times. Now fear was producing a kind of spiritual amnesia in my heart and I was struggling to recall His faithfulness. My heart was stalled, projecting onto the screen of my mind a future that was more than I could handle. No doubt about it, I had been running a good race but I was growing weary. The dizziness was wearing me down. All this was going through my mind as I sat there alone on my birthday with my peace shattered and my fear alive and well.

So what did I do about it? I decided to open a birthday present. After all, dizzy or not, it was my birthday and I thought a present might be just the thing to get my mind off my troubles. My sister in law had given me her family's birthday present on Christmas Eve to take home with me. I reached under the Christmas tree and pulled it out.

Getting into the spirit of things, I tore off the ribbon and paper and opened the box. My sister in law had asked me a few weeks earlier what I wanted for my birthday. I told her I'd been looking for a throw or small blanket with green and blue in it to place on the back of my couch. Unable to find one myself, I thought she might have better luck. I added that a simple pair of earrings would be great as well, in case her search ended like mine.

Pulling off the wrapping paper and reaching into the box, I found a charming throw. It had birds of both green and blue stitched across it with a lovely background of flowers of the same color. Stitched in exquisite letters across the body of the small blanket was the following:

Look at the birds of the air. They neither sow nor reap nor store away in barns yet your heavenly Father cares for them. Therefore, do not worry about tomorrow. Matthew 6

I was shocked. Tears gathered in my eyes, rising quickly and without warning. How could this be? At the very moment when I could no longer picture facing my tomorrows successfully, I received a present that literally, and I mean literally, told me that I should not worry about tomorrow. My sister in law did not know about the struggle I was going through. Later I learned that she found my present at the local Ace Hardware where they decided to temporarily sell these items in their gift shop. When I investigated the following week to see if they had any more, they told me they had sold out and had no plans to carry that product in the future.

I felt the words on the blanket go right into my heart. If Psalm 107 contained a promise that God understood my situation and would lead me to a place of healing, then the scripture from Matthew 6 was a command, telling me how to live until the Psalm's promise was fulfilled.

For the first time that day I thought to myself, "I can do this. I can keep going and live in this day, trusting that God will help me live in tomorrow when tomorrow comes."

It was nothing short of a revelation to my weary heart, a survival plan, a map through uncharted territory. I felt then that I could keep going if I took into account the words that had come my way. From that point on, living between the promise and the command became a rallying theme for me. Every day as I woke and the worries of my upcoming week advanced across the screen of my mind, I reminded myself to stay focused on that one day and His provision for me. Time after time I came back to my marching orders. Like the birds I was unable to sow and reap and store in barns, but God had promised to provide. All I had to do was stop worrying and start trusting.

During this time an interesting thing happened. I was invited to speak six different times at local job networking groups held in churches all over the city. These were places where people who had lost their jobs during the current recession went to look for help with their job search. It occurred to me fairly quickly that there was a parallel between the dizziness of vertigo and the way your life gets off balance when you experience any crisis, especially the loss of a job. In both cases things change dramatically. You feel out of control, worried about future demands, and wonder whether you will be able to meet those demands in your current state. I began sharing the message that there is a way to live in scary times and that God has promised His presence, His provision and eventually a haven for us. He has given us a way to survive the trip. I called the presentation, *Finding a Job is a Journey*. I could just as easily have called it *Surviving Vertigo is a Journey*. You probably have a name you could slot in there as well. We are all going somewhere and everyone's road seems to have a fair amount of bumps in it.

About a month ago I spoke at the last of my current engagements for job networking groups. The week before, after six months of either spinning or daily dizziness, I had my first whole day without feeling dizzy. It was only one day but I was beginning to feel real progress and an entire day without dizziness was heaven to me. The three weeks to three months estimate for my recovery had been way off just as the time it was taking many of these people to find jobs had long exceeded their estimate. One man had been looking for work for eighteen months. I don't think I could have spoken to him of hope had I not just been through the discipline of walking in it every day for so many months. When he left, my prayer for him was that he could and would continue his journey until he found his own haven.

I'm still struggling some. Got a bug of some sort this week and the dizziness came back after a two week absence. But I'm beginning to think that life really is a lot more about the journey than the destination. Don't get me wrong. I want to reach my refuge and if I had it my way, I'd have arrived there yesterday. Still, as my sister says, "progress, not perfection."

In the meantime I'm keeping in mind that I have a way to keep going until I arrive at the safe haven God has promised me; hope in His provision today and believe in His promise to lead me to calm waters in His time. Feel free to try it for yourself. It's as simple as living between the Promise and the Command.

THE DOGGY DOOR

I heard the scratching at the door and looked up. From my perch at the café styled kitchen table where I was working on my computer, I could see her face. It was pitiful. Large brown eyes, round and innocent, looked up at me from the other side of the glass door. They were almost pleading, begging me to consider her case. Couldn't I just let her in? Her two front paws rested against the step and her tiny white body, smudged all over with big black spots in varying shapes, shook. She is genuinely talented at shaking on demand so I didn't take it too seriously. She shakes when I leave in the morning every day, only stopping long enough to run to the front window and bark like crazy once I step out the door. I knew she wanted to come in but I refused to get up and go to the door. What could possibly cause such a callous response on my part to such an innocent request on hers?

"Go to your door," I called out to the small rat terrier, pointing to the doggie door just around the corner from her current position. "Go on, girl! You can do it. Come in your door."

Nothing. She sat and stared harder leaning her head to the side, scratching again and waiting for a response from me. If dogs could plead, she did. Why wouldn't I come to her? It was only a few steps and now her shaking was getting worse.

"Casey Lou," I said to her, more sternly this time, "Go to your door. Look! It's right there. Come on in. Come here, girl!" I wasn't sure if I was begging or demanding but it didn't seem to matter because the dog was standing her ground, refusing to budge from her current position.

I was starting to get aggravated. For the last month I had fed Casey treats of every kind in an attempt to teach her to push open the little door and jump through. We had also put beautiful octagonal shaped steps right outside her new entrance so she could step directly from the kitchen on to level ground. In other words, we had made her new doggie door both easy and rewarding to use.

We had taken pains to train her to use this new device. Every day we had gone into the yard and called to her from directly outside the door, bribing her with a juicy morsel to come out. Once she relented and came into the yard, I had gone back inside and offered her more treats to come through in the opposite direction. It was hamburger that finally did the trick. Casey Lou will go anywhere to get a piece of hamburger.

Eventually she got the gist of all this coming in and out through a small hole in the wall and food was no longer required. Casey Lou seemed to realize she had gained the freedom to run outside and chase squirrels any time she chose. It was a revelation for her! It wasn't long before she could be seen leaping through the doggie door at a run, racing across the yard at full speed in hopes of catching an unsuspecting bird or chipmunk. She hasn't caught one yet but she seems to thrive on the chase. She's especially fond of going after chipmunks, which have a tendency to go underground as soon as they see her coming. In testimony to this obsession of hers, you can see a huge hole under my air conditioning unit where Casey has spent hours trying to dig out some of the elusive little creatures.

So why was she sitting there at the back door, whining and begging as if she had been abandoned and neglected on the back step? Why didn't she just walk the few steps around the corner and come on in? After all, this dog had free access to warmth and food whenever she wanted. Why would she exile herself from the comfort of the house when it was hers to have at will?

"Treat!" I called with sudden inspiration. I got up from the table, went back to the cabinet and pulled out a piece of carrot covered with dried chicken (yes, they do have treats like that) and held it up.

Immediately the tiny head disappeared and within a few seconds it reappeared, her small body exploding through the doggie door, a delighted grin on her face. She was at my feet with tail wagging in no time at all. Leaning down I patted her and gave her the treat. I try to be a realist. I was working and Casey was annoying me with her unnecessary scratching at the back door. If I needed a treat to remind her how to use her new entrance, I was willing to pay the price. Casey was inside the house and I could return to my work. Plus, I had won the battle and gotten her to use her new entrance rather than opening the door for her.

Still, this episode got me thinking. I understand the lure of a treat. After all, I've been known to drive several miles for a home baked brownie and even further for chocolate cake with ice cream. Yes, sirreee! I recognize the lure of good food to make a body move. What I'm confused about is why a body, human or animal, would sit voluntarily in the freezing cold when there is easy access to warmth and friends a few feet away.

Casey knew how to get in the house. She had been using her new door regularly for several weeks now. Granted, until it had been put in, she had entered and exited the house through the large glass door facing the back yard. She was used to having someone open the glass door for her, used to her old routine. Did she just forget momentarily that there was a newer, faster way to get what she wanted? Or was she simply distracted because she could see me through the window? Did what was right in front of her make her forget her options, make her forget she could have what she wanted with a few simple steps to the right?

I think Casey Lou is a lot like you and me. She is used to a certain routine. Even though she now has new freedom and new options, she has spent a fair amount of time in the past pawing, waiting, and using her persuasive puppy eyes to call for help. She is used to sitting in front of an obstacle and letting someone else remove it. So even though she's been given a new and better way, she sometimes gets distracted by old habits and what she sees right in front of her through the glass door. She seems to temporarily forget that she has a new and better way to get inside any time she wants.

It reminds me of all the times I've been through something hard in my life, learned a lesson from it in my heart and spirit, and found new freedom in God. Then, the next thing you know I have spiritual amnesia. Suddenly I forget what I have learned, forget God's faithfulness, and I am instead distracted by my old habits and fears.

John, a friend of mine, recently shared a story with me about his father that illustrates this phenomenon perfectly. His dad, a veteran of the Korean War, began acting strangely a few years ago. He and

John's mother had two homes. One was a vacation home passed down through the generations. It sits on the Maine shore and in the winter the family uses it for easy access to skiing, while in the summer, they vacation on the beautiful, wild beaches. It wasn't unusual for his father to go up to the beach house, only a few hours from where they lived, to do some much needed chores. But over the past year or so, his father had been spending more time at the beach house than anywhere else. Once, when he did come home, John noticed a strange smell about him and began to wonder. Was his father depressed, pulling away from the family and not taking care of himself? Could that be what was causing the odd smell? Determined to get to the bottom of what was going on, John asked his father about it. The answer was evasive and his father quickly escaped the conversation by going into the other room. John let it go, deciding maybe it was nothing after all.

Eventually Christmas came. John's father called his mother and announced he would be spending Christmas at the vacation house. As you can imagine, mom was having none of it. She insisted he come home and spend the holidays with his family. Reluctantly he agreed. When his father returned, he finally broke down and told his wife what he had been so carefully hiding.

"I'm dying," he told her. "I have cancer and its growing."

He raised his sleeve and John's mother saw a large growth on his arm that had wrapped its way around a bicep. John's mother is a nurse and she had only to take one look at her husband's arm to know he had basil cell skin cancer. The normal treatment for a small basil cell cancer is fairly simple and when treated early, recovery is normally easy and complete. John's father had let his condition fester for so long he required extensive surgery and a skin graft in order to remedy the situation. The good news is that he eventually let his wife convince him to take care of it.

Asking his father why he'd let the growth get so big, John learned that, as a child, his dad had a bad experience in a hospital. He was deathly afraid of going to one for treatment. When he had first noticed the growth he avoided it instead of dealing with it. Then he isolated himself from his family, hoping to find healing in the waters off the Maine coast.

His fear almost killed him. Like Casey, his habitual response to finding safety didn't involve doing anything new. Surely he knew his wife, a nurse, could have gotten him the help he needed. Like Casey, he had a new door that he could easily access. But old habits and fears die hard and he was willing to stay outside the family to avoid them. When confronted with his fear of hospitals, he chose to risk death and look for his own cure rather than try something new. His hope in something new wasn't as strong as his fear of the past.

God has promised to provide for us in our daily journey. Many times He has already provided an answer for us but we forget about it or refuse it. A couple I know recently separated. The wife offered to keep her husband on her health insurance so he could have some much needed medical coverage until they decided whether to divorce. He refused her offer even though he had no insurance of his own. At the time he was in physical therapy for a hurt back. He couldn't afford to get well without her help but still, he refused.

 Instead, he asked her forgiveness for all he had done to hurt her in the marriage. She agreed to forgive him if he would put aside his pride and accept the medical coverage until he could get some of his own. He refused again. The irony is that until they actually divorced or open enrollment occurred at the end of the year, his wife could not remove him from her health plan anyway. But for quite some time he refused to accept the provision offered. He, like Casey, had trouble learning to accept and use a gift that was presented to him. Like John's father, he risked his health before trying a new way.

We're not so different from Casey Lou. We have short memories and can miss or refuse the provision of God. We hold on to our old habits and then complain that we don't have what we need. So what do you do if you find yourself in a similar predicament?

If you want the hope that comes from knowing God provides, you might just need to use the doggie door. There could be a tasty treat waiting on the other side. Even if you don't like hamburger as much as Casey Lou, you will have access to a warm, safe place.

It only takes a few steps and a small push.

PEACE LAMBS

I once had a boss who called me Barbara.

"Barbara, figure out how to do that and get back to me, will you?" she'd suggest sweetly.

She was very big on getting us to figure out how to do things and then doing them. I know that sounds healthy on the surface; like the ability to delegate appropriately or maybe like a hands-off management style, preferred by a wide range of employees universally. However, there was a glitch in this system. Things just seemed to spiral out of control whenever you were bold enough to ask a question about how to get something done. The next thing you know you were in charge of an entire project you didn't know how to do and your current team members had been asked to form a brand new team with you so everyone could figure out how to complete the project together. Worst of all, your original question more than likely remained unanswered.

For instance if you said something like, "How do you plan to communicate that new policy?" she would inevitably say, "Barbara, will you please figure that out and get back to me with the plan, finished communication pieces and timeline by noon tomorrow?" Again, she would smile sweetly and move quickly on to the next topic. Something just wasn't right. Eventually, we all learned to stop asking those pesky questions.

Ah, well. In the end, all the hyper-delegating and tricky question answering seemed minor compared to the fact that I just cringed every time she called my name, or rather, every time she called me

Barbara. You see, my name is Jan. That's right, Jan. Not Barbara. If you think about it for even a moment, you will realize that those names aren't even vaguely similar. It was as if I were a completely different person once she arrived on the scene, not the Jan I had been all those years before she showed up. If you are thinking that you aren't that great at remembering names either, I feel your pain. I struggle in that area too. However, I have made a point to remember the names of those who report directly to me, even if I can't remember everyone else. It just seems like the obvious thing to do.

What made things worse for me in all this was that my boss seemed perfectly capable of remembering her other direct reports, consistently calling out each of their names correctly. She did call another team member Laura a few times, but her name was Laurie so at least that was close. No one was being called Jan. I was beginning to have a distinctly uneasy feeling about the probability of a productive relationship with this new manager of mine.

I don't want to misrepresent what was happening. She didn't always call me Barbara—only every third or fourth time she addressed me. The other members of our team caught on to what was happening and starting calling me Barbara Jan, in reference to the Beach Boy's song, Barbara Ann. Occasionally they just couldn't keep in their amusement, laughing out loud once during a meeting when the mysterious name calling occurred. This caused my boss to hesitate momentarily and look at us in apparent confusion.

"You called her Barbara!" said one of my laughing co-workers in response to her puzzled look.

"Oh, did I do that again? I keep doing that, don't I?" she replied and then continued on with her agenda of getting us to figure out how to do things. It was at that point that I stopped hoping for an apology or even an acknowledgement that the habit was not only annoying but potentially rude. After all, I sat in the office right next door to her, she only had seven direct reports, and she had spent her entire first day in a classroom with me standing in front of her helping her to get familiar with our company. Shouldn't that have counted for something in the name remembering department?

To put all this in perspective, let me tell you a little story. One year, when I was a child, I'd been given three tiny ducklings for Easter. I loved those little ducks and named them Hewey, Dewey and Louie. Every day when I came home from school I would run to the back yard and get them out of their cage. Then we would go for long walks through the woods near the house. How did I keep us all together you may wonder? I just started walking and they all followed right behind me in a little row. Apparently in a new environment, whatever or whoever you come across early in your journey, makes an "impression" on you so that a kind of bonding occurs. It seems I impressed myself on the little ducklings and, as a result, we could march together as well as a highly trained military unit. That's why I was a little surprised that not only had I not made an impression on my new boss, I had made an impression for someone named Barbara. I guess corporate America is a little short on the bonding instinct.

I eventually left the company. Friends and co-workers looked at me worriedly and asked, "Why are you leaving?" and I responded simply, "She calls me Barbara." After all, what else was there to say?

I did throw in that I was going to write a book but I'm pretty sure no one, including me, thought this story would be in it.

Today I'm sitting in a bookstore cafe and have been discreetly watching an unusual duo sitting side by side at two small tables against the wall. There is a slightly older man, with a book and a cup of coffee in front of him. He is half reclining, with his feet on the chair in front of him and one arm across the back of the bench on which he sits. Right next to him, at her own small table, is a young woman, maybe a college student, who also sits casually with her feet on a chair and a computer in front of her. She is slouching over the computer a little, as if she were working on it in bed instead of in a café. He is talking, apparently to her. There is no one else around and their elbows are practically touching. She is looking at her computer, eyes glued to the screen, fingers poking slowly at the keys. Not once has she looked in his direction nor he in hers. Yet, he is talking rapidly with barely an occasional pause in his ongoing monologue. He is smiling so I'm assuming it's an entertaining conversation.

All this makes me ponder how we connect with others. Have the busy rush of life and the onset of the age of technology made it unnecessary to remember peoples' names or to look at them when you talk to them? Have I missed an important transition in our culture where now people sit side by side without knowing each other's names and carry on a "conversation?" I know it's a waste of time to judge these things. Communication is a fragile business at best and we all stumble at times.

I, too, recently almost missed something very important in a conversation with a wonderful person at work. Just because I remember the names of my direct reports and try to look at people when they are talking to me, doesn't mean that I don't sometimes mess things up, too. My friend's name is…well, let's just call him Ted for now. That's not his real name but then, does it really matter?

Ted and I had been with the same company for years and had many opportunities to work together on projects. The week before I was to leave the company, Ted came to see me. It was clear he was concerned about my leaving and my well-being, I suppose because I had been with the company for so long. He knew it was a big change for me and was wondering what I would do to fill my time, find a new routine and start a new life. Also, he wanted me to know how much he valued what we had accomplished together.

"If you ever have a bad day out there, a day when you aren't sure if you are valued or aren't sure which way to go, I want you to remember how much you have helped me and my team while you were here. This company is a better place because of the work you've done with us," he told me sincerely. By the way, he was looking me in the eye when he said it which helped me to believe he meant what he was saying.

I thanked him for the kind words and told him not to worry. During my previous year I had been learning to trust God and live one day at a time. My experiences, though not pleasant, had helped prepare me for the big change of leaving my job. As I was telling him the specifics of what had happened to cause this realization, he suddenly looked at me and said, "I have a very similar story. Would you like to hear it?"

Would I like to hear it?! I live for the words "I have a story" because this is where I find God most often—in stories that live right in the neighborhood or at work or sometimes on the plane or in a cab.

"Yes!" I said excitedly.

He looked at me and began his story. "Recently my family and I went to Hawaii for vacation," Ted said. I have to admit that I was immediately a wee bit jealous thinking of the swaying palm trees and lovely beaches. I recovered quickly from this little distraction with some eye contact and a nod of the head, indicating he should continue.

"One day," he said, "we changed hotels and somewhere along the line I realized that my daughter had left her swimsuit at our previous location. After calling the old hotel to confirm that they did indeed have the suit, I jumped in the car and headed out over unfamiliar streets to retrieve it. At some point the car in front of me got my attention." He paused. "Actually, it wasn't a car but rather a van of some sort; not like a Fed Ex vehicle but more like a local furniture delivery van. Something was written across the back of the truck. When we stopped at the light I took a second to read it. **Peace Lambs 91** it said." Ted was getting ready to go on when I interrupted.

"Peace lambs?" I asked, sure that I was missing something important here. I scrolled through my brain to see if I could find any connection with this little phrase but nothing came to mind. "Peace lambs?" I asked again.

"Yes," he said. "You know, like Psalms only with the letters mixed up."

When he saw my blank look, he spelled it out for me. "P-s-l-a-m-s. P-Slams."

Talk about a misunderstanding! I was picturing tiny sheep bleating calmly while he was talking about the Bible. The mix-up may be more explainable than Barbara vs. Jan, but nevertheless, there it was. What's more is that it happened even though I was sitting right across from him maintaining eye contact and giving him my undivided attention—well, except for the part about daydreaming of going to Hawaii.

"Ah," I responded. "So you saw something on a truck about a Psalm?"

"Yes, and I immediately felt that it was something important to me personally and that I should go home and read it. When I got back to the hotel with the swim suit, I picked up my Bible and read Psalm 91. The whole psalm is beautiful but verses 14 and 15 seemed to lodge in my heart unexpectedly."

Ted pulled out his iPhone and looked up the Psalm on his Holy Bible App. This is what he read:

"Because he loves me," says the Lord, "I will rescue him; I will protect him, for he acknowledges my name. He will call

upon me, and I will answer him; I will be with him in trouble, I will deliver and honor him."

Ted read with passion and then looked up at me and said, "God said that because I acknowledged Him He was going to honor me. I couldn't get over it. Love me, maybe, but honor me? And when I was in trouble? I wasn't having any trouble that I knew of but the message was loud and clear. Whatever was coming up, God had rescue plans in place."

The next day, while relaxing at the hotel, Ted got a call from a contact back home.

"I heard from someone in our industry that there is a confidential recruitment search out for your job," his friend told him. "It looks like your boss is trying to replace you while you are on vacation. I hate to call you like this but I thought you might want to know."

Stunned at the news, Ted thanked his friend and hung up the phone. He was thousands of miles from home, on a well-earned rest with his family, and he had just learned that he would probably be replaced in his job when he returned to the States.

"I've never been a confrontational type of person, Jan. You know that."

When he called me by my real name, it was music to my ears. Funny how you can take the little things for granted.

"I like to get things done but I don't like conflict. However, I knew I would have to do something when I returned. I would have to confront my boss. I couldn't just sit around and wait to be informed about my fate," he said. "I immediately thought of the words I had seen on the back of the delivery truck. They had led me to read a message, a Psalm that assured me that God would honor me and rescue me from trouble. I knew in my heart that I would have to engage in some uncomfortable conversations when I went back to work but it seemed God had a handle on the situation. I spent a fair amount of time during the rest of my vacation thinking about it."

"When I returned to work, I continued to wonder how to begin the dialogue with my boss. I am a planner. Usually I plan my conversations—I don't like to go in cold or unprepared. I need to know what I want to say in advance and I even like to have a back-up plan," Ted said, looking away a little and remembering.

"But no matter how much I thought about it, I just couldn't figure out a good way to approach this. I kept going back to Psalm 91—'I will rescue him, I will protect him, I will be with him in trouble, and I will honor him,' is what the Lord had spoken to me through His Word."

"I prayed, repeated the scriptures, and finally went into my boss' office and told him what I had found out. He was surprised and, it seemed, sorry that I discovered all this from someone other than himself. However, once the topic was on the table, we had a calm conversation. He acknowledged he didn't want our parting to be immediate or on bad terms and agreed to work with me on when and how I would leave. I'm happy to say the company has been fair to me during the transition."

Ted took a deep breath and said, "I'll be leaving in about a month. My wife and I have decided to take some time off and ask God to show us what is next before we make any plans."

I could see he was uneasy facing the unknown. My heart went out to him. Still, I figured if God had taken the time to communicate with Ted on the streets of Hawaii, He would be sure to help him move on to the next phase of his life.

Ted glowed when he told his story. He was amazed at the way things unfolded for him and after listening to his adventure, I added 'the back of a truck' to my list of unusual places from which God speaks to us.

I guess in the long run it doesn't matter whether your boss at work remembers your name, looks at you when they speak, or puts out a search to replace you while you are on vacation. There is a God who knows your name and He knows just where you are and what you will need. There is no place you can go where He cannot find you and no battle you must face that He is not aware of. When you get the nudge that He is speaking to you, get off the computer and listen. You might want to make eye contact with some of His works—like a beautiful sunset, a bird in flight or maybe even a Peace Lamb.

God has promised to provide for us. Sometimes He even gives us our daily bread on the back of a delivery truck, so pay attention. If you listen when He speaks, you can't help but find hope.

Hope. Now that is a name worth remembering.

Chapter 4

The Fourth Promise of Hope:

His Participation

We hope in His Participation.
Hope tells us that God meets us where we are—in the everyday moments of our lives.

"O Lord, you have searched me and you know me. You know when I sit and when I rise; you perceive my thoughts from afar. You discern my going out and my lying down; you are familiar with all my ways."

Psalm 139: 1-3

A MATCH MADE IN HEAVEN

I first noticed it out of the corner of my eye. It was just a small white blur on the street outside my window and I didn't pay much attention. It wasn't until the second time when I caught the movement in my peripheral vision that I stopped what I was doing to investigate. From my vantage point in the kitchen, I could see both the street in front of my house and the trees in the back. I'd always loved that view. Not only was it beautiful but I could easily see anyone approaching my house. Today the view simply wasn't enough to adequately warn me of what was headed my way.

The white blur had aroused my curiosity. As I turned to look closer, the form came into focus. It was nothing but a small dog trotting up the street. What was interesting was that after the animal disappeared from view, it was only a few short minutes before the little creature trotted right back past the window again headed in the other direction. I waited a few more minutes to see what would happen and sure enough, there it came again, having turned around to trot up the street going the other way.

I couldn't tell what breed it was, only that its color was dingy white and its coat puffy and rough, like the unkempt, wool of a young lamb in winter. It moved with a precise pace, changing direction only once it reached the end of the street. You'd have thought the little animal was leading a parade, with its head held high and its forward progress made consistently in a straight line. Back and forth it went, up and down the street, looking to each side as it made its rounds of the neighborhood.

It appeared to be nodding at some invisible fans or maybe it was looking for something. I wondered momentarily if it was lost.

Just then a friend of mine, busy talking on her cell phone, pulled her car up on the street in front of the house. We were going to a meeting that evening and I figured she would come inside when she finished her call. Forgetting the small dog, I went back to my work in the kitchen and waited for my friend to come to the door. It wasn't long before I heard her knock and enter.

"Do you have any dog food?" Bree asked, not wasting any time on formalities as she poked her head around the corner of the kitchen.

Despite not owning an animal of my own, I kept extra dog food on hand for the times I watched my daughter's miniature rat terrier, Casey Lou. Bree must have seen the look on my face as she asked for some dog food and was quick to explain.

"A cute little dog came up to my car a minute ago and put its paws on the door. Then, when I opened the door it ran away and wouldn't come near me. I think it looks a little thin though. Maybe we could feed it," she explained, excited to play a part in the dog's unexplained journey.

"Uh, I don't think we should feed it," I replied. "I'm sure if we leave it alone, it will go home to its real owners soon enough. If you feed it, don't you own it? I think there is actually some legal principle that applies in these situations. Don't they say possession is nine tenths of the law?"

She looked at me skeptically. While I like to think of myself as dog friendly, I had a funny foreboding about this furry pooch. Bree pressed on, undaunted by my response.

"What if it doesn't have a home? What if it's lost? You know that it is going to get cold tonight and the least we can do is to fortify it just in case. Don't you agree?"

I didn't, really. I mean, I was starting to feel like we should get going and I really didn't think it was a good idea to feed a stray dog. I wasn't convinced it would eat the food anyway. It hadn't stopped its relentless march up and down the street the whole time we'd been talking. On the other hand, I didn't want the little animal to go hungry. And after all, what could it hurt to give it a little dog food?

Finally I decided feeding the dog fell into the category of helping one of God's creatures, thinking that what goes around comes around. I was pretty sure the principle held true even though the other day after doing something kind for a total stranger, I immediately tripped over a basket left in a store aisle by a challenged shopper. Then as I was leaving the story I almost fell off the curb. I guess sometimes you have to wait awhile for that stuff to come back around.

I asked my friend to put the dish, which I filled to the brim, out by the curb. I hoped that if we left the food at the end of the driveway instead of at my back door, the dog could easily access it without getting too attached. I was seeing this charitable effort as more of a jog-by eating event than a sit down meal. If all went well, the pup would barely have to veer off its designated path to grab a few bites on its way home. Kind of like a doggy drive-through.

So out went the bowl of food, right on the curb near the mailbox. I noticed the animal trot by and I thought again that this was a dog on a mission, not one to be deterred by the lure of food. It was time to leave so Bree and I got into my car and headed down the driveway toward the street. At that moment two things happened simultaneously.

The little dog veered from the road onto my lawn and headed toward the food bowl. At the same moment, my friend, who saw the dog approaching the food, opened the car door and called out to it in her most convincing puppy prattle.

"Come here, little doggie! Come on!" she sing-songed across the lawn. She patted her knee and gave the animal her biggest smile.

"Bree," I said, "close the door! What are you doing? You are going to fall out of the car!"

OK. So, we were barely moving and there was little chance of falling out without landing on the lawn. That didn't mean opening the car door and calling to a strange dog was a good idea, did it? What was my friend thinking? Why would this animal approach her now while she was in a moving car when it wouldn't come to her earlier in a car that was perfectly still? What happened next took us both by surprise.

Without further encouragement the dog changed direction, headed away from the bowl of food, trotted alongside the car and jumped in, landing squarely on Bree's lap. We were both so stunned we couldn't speak. It proceeded to sniff her, jumped on to the front floor to sniff there for a moment and then launched itself into the back seat and lay down. The next thing we knew it was curled up and settled in for the ride.

I've often wondered if it knew we were headed toward a small group Bible Study.

After a few minutes the little dog got up and leaned forward, front paws perched on the area between the two front seats, back paws resting against the rear seat. This was a dog used to being a part of what was going on. I think if it could have spoken it would have joined in the conversation.

"Wow, thanks!" I pictured it saying. "Cold enough to freeze a puppy's paws out there. Where are we going?"

Of course it said nothing but simply looked from side to side, watching as we drove down the early winter streets with the dark settling in.

"What are we going to do with this dog?" I asked Bree. A distinct dog smell was starting to be noticeable and I decided it had been quite some time since the pup had been bathed. I was wondering how the others would react to her once we reached our destination. I say "her" at this point because it only took us a minute to discover "it" was a "she" once she joined us in the car.

"We'll take her in with us," Bree beamed.

Bree hadn't owned a dog in a long time and I guess her cats weren't doing it for her. You would think she'd just been given a valentine from her favorite beau or won the big lotto prize the way she smiled back at our little hitchhiker.

"We can see if someone there wants to keep her," she said excitedly.

Despite my concerns, my friend assured me that it would all work out. As we pulled up in front of the small house, Bree ran in to tell the group of our dilemma and returned saying the owner had agreed to let the dog stay in his garage while we met. Unfortunately, to get to the garage I had to go through the main room, completely disrupting the meeting that had already begun. Several of the people there enthusiastically greeted our small interloper. A few even made comments about how they wished they had room for another animal at their place. For a minute, I felt hope flicker in my heart. Maybe we would find a home for this dog after all.

After putting her in the garage and closing the door, I sat down and the meeting picked back up where it had left off. It wasn't more than a couple of minutes before we heard a strange sound from the behind the garage door. Everyone stopped and listened as the dog howled a little and then scratched at the door. I blushed.

"I'm sure she will quiet down in a minute," I stammered, looking down at my feet. "Go ahead. Just ignore her."

The leader continued his lesson and almost immediately the tiny animal escalated its noisy scratching and whining. After several more minutes of the same, I was finally forced to go and get her. For lack of any other idea, I decided to put her on my lap, assuring everyone I would keep her still and quiet. I only hoped that I could. Then we continued with the evening's agenda. The discussion provided another surprise in my unusual day.

If I hadn't known better, I'd have thought that the little dog, whom we were now calling Lambkins due to her unkempt wooly look, understood Scripture. Every time someone read or discussed something from the Good Book she looked at them as if enthralled. Was she familiar with our topic or was she just too tired to jump off my lap and look for a cat to chase? Whenever someone made an insightful comment about our study material, she appeared to ponder them approvingly. I began trying to remember what I had learned about a "hound of heaven" from my literature class. While I was pretty sure it didn't refer to an actual canine, I thought it might be an apt description of our furry visitor.

By the time we finished and everyone was ready to leave for the evening, there were still no real takers for Lambkins. My friend and I got into the car with the fuzzy, slightly smudged pooch perched comfortably between us and started home.

So, what next? I thought. I knew Bree had no room for a dog. She lived in a small apartment with two cats and limited space. It was clear she couldn't keep the dog that she'd so enthusiastically enticed into my car. No one at our meeting appeared to be able to keep her either. The options were definitely looking limited.

I started wondering. You know how there are certain sounds only animals can hear, like the high pitch of a dog whistle? Was it possible that my house emitted a sound we human's couldn't hear that invited wayward animals to drop by and hang out with me? Lambkins' stopover wasn't the only experience I'd had with an uninvited visitor from the animal kingdom. The first one had been with a pregnant feline named Miss Kitty who insisted that we were friends despite my allergy to all things catlike. Now I had to decide what to do with my latest unsolicited guest.

It didn't take long to figure out that the most important thing I could do that evening was to introduce Lambkins to bathwater and a little shampoo. Recruiting my friend to help me bathe the dog, we cleaned and blow-dried her in no time at all. Bree had to leave soon after and, as I watched her drive away, I felt a wave of anxiety wash over me. What if I couldn't find the pup's owner or someone who wanted her? Dog-sitting for Casey Lou was my first allegiance and I wasn't ready to include another animal in my life right now. Don't get me wrong, it's wasn't that I didn't like Lambkins. I did. But for some reason I couldn't explain, my heart just wasn't into claiming her as my own.

I turned from my worries to take a closer look at the little dog. She was cute and I guessed she was a small poodle of some sort. Now that she was clean and dry, her coat was whiter and the somewhat unkempt, curls cascading all over her were very endearing. Sort of like a poodle Orphan Annie, I thought.

Taking her out to the backyard, I quickly realized that she was house trained as well. After our jaunt outside, we returned to the kitchen and set up a doggie bed, some water, and a bowl of food for her. I put up an old baby gate to keep her in the kitchen and headed off to bed. When I woke in the morning, there she sat in her little bed, wagging her tail and looking at me expectantly. She'd been no problem during the night. I was relieved and decided my doubts from the evening before were nothing after all.

That day I worked from my home office so I could keep an eye on her. After telling my staff about Lambkins over the phone, they decided to come over for lunch at a nearby restaurant so they could drop by and check out my doggie visitor.

"She's perfect for you!" they gushed once they'd arrived and had a chance to look at her. "You need a dog and she showed up right on your doorstep. What more could you ask for? Look at her. She is so cute!"

They each leaned over and patted Lambkin's newly washed fur. She looked like a toy store lamb at this point, with her big brown eyes, sweet face, and ears at half-mast poking out from under a fully blown coat of puffy, white fur.

"I don't need a dog right now," I said, trying to stand firm against their unexpected mutiny.

The enthusiastic desire to match people with dates and dogs is something many people jump into with nothing short of the passion of true love itself. It doesn't seem to matter to them that they have absolutely no qualifications for the task. Nor do they think that you might consider what they are doing to be meddling in your life. So the numerous comments I heard over the next few days shouldn't have surprised me. Friends, family and even strangers commented that the universe, fate, and karma had brought this tiny creature to my front door to fill my life with her curly hair and sweet doggy love. I wasn't fooled. The people declaring that my newest love had arrived were the same people who had told me in the past that they knew just the right man for me as well.

"Yes, Gary, that's it! Oh, you two are perfect for each other! I don't know why I didn't think of it before," my well-meaning friends would say.

However, after a dinner with the mystery man and several hours of listening to him proclaim his achievements as well as his ex-wife's flaws, it was clear to me that my matchmakers' love meters were out of whack. To keep from getting derailed on this controversial topic of helping your friends and neighbors find true love, let me just say that simply because someone I don't know, man or mutt, is guided to my door by a caring friend, it is not a clear indicator that love is imminent. Still, I do believe that both people and animals are guided to our doors for a reason, even if it isn't forever love. I don't think the "universe" actually has thoughts of its own, but I do believe that the Maker of the universe does. I just wished I knew what He was thinking at that moment.

As for Lambkins, I made posters and put them up all over the neighborhood and in the small town nearby trying to find her real owners. Some part of me was sure that she was simply lost and that someone would show up soon to claim her. I tried to forget about the stories I had heard of animals cruelly abandoned when their "families" moved and no longer wanted a pet. She really was a nice little dog and I was wondering why anyone would leave her on purpose.

I noticed that as the dog was becoming more comfortable with her surroundings her personality was starting to emerge. She liked to turn in circles on her hind legs like a circus animal while making little noises in the process. The slight dizziness I felt while watching her faded quickly enough. "Hmm," I thought. Nevertheless, she was cute and endearing and my hope meter for her was on full throttle.

I penned Lambkins in the kitchen on the second morning and went off to work. When I returned home that evening she was so happy to see me she started turning in circles and whining almost immediately. I sat down and closed my eyes for a minute, rubbing them with my fingers to ease the dizzy feeling. When I opened them she was sitting down, looking at me expectantly. I gave her chicken for dinner that night in hopes of lulling her to sleep with a full tummy.

That night Lambkins managed to escape from the kitchen by spinning the baby gate on its side, like a pig on a spit. Slipping under it she found a better spot on a big chair in the den. When I found her there, I put her back in the kitchen. It wasn't long before she escaped again and this time she came to my bedroom door. I was aware that with each break out, the dog was slowly making her way closer to my room. But I was standing strong. No matter what everyone else suggested, I had no intention of sharing my bed with a stranger—even one with floppy ears and soft fur.

Like a worm on a hook, I was beginning to think that I might get swallowed while helping this little dog catch the right owner. I wondered if I was meant to keep her like my friends had suggested. Was she sent to my door to stay? Lambkins was a great little dog but my heart belonged to Casey Lou. Apparently I was a one dog woman—and a part time one at that. I started praying in earnest that God would help me with my dilemma. What should I do? While everyone else thought we made the perfect couple, I couldn't see myself making a lifetime commitment to Lambkins.

The next morning I admitted to myself that I could no longer keep Lambkins penned in the kitchen. She was able to roam the house at will. That meant I needed to come home at lunch time and let her out in the yard. When I got to work that morning I looked at my calendar and saw that I had a luncheon date scheduled with a friend of mine, KC. I would need to cancel it, I thought. I hated to leave my friend in the lurch as I had already cancelled twice before due to business demands. Not knowing what else to do, I picked up the phone and called her.

"KC, I'm so sorry," I said when she answered the phone. "I have a stray dog at my house and I need to go home and let her out at lunch time. Turns out I can't keep her contained in the kitchen and I don't want her to be stuck all day without a potty break. Can we reschedule lunch again?"

I hesitated for a moment before I added, "That is unless you want to get some lunch at a drive-through and then take a ride with me to the other side of town to watch this dog go to the bathroom." It never occurred to me that she might take me up on the offer.

"Oh, I'd love to go!" she said without hesitation.

KC is a truly unique friend, an incredibly talented artist who does creative work for our company and helps me out when there is a need for a book cover or logo. She is fun and open and loves anything that is out of the ordinary. So the idea of a fast food lunch along with the opportunity to pat a lost dog sounded like a great adventure to her.

I was relieved that I didn't have to cancel on her and glad to have her company as we made our way toward my house. Once we arrived, we went in and immediately opened the back door for Lambkins. Following her outside, I breathed in the fresh air. It was a lovely day. Maybe this little trip wasn't going to be so bad after all.

KC had some sort of chemistry with Lambkins right from the start. She patted her and cooed at her and called her by name. When Lambkins started her spinning routine accompanied by her little noise, KC thought it was precious. She didn't close her eyes even once during the twirling like I had. As KC played with the dog, she began telling me about a dog of her own.

"About two months ago, my little dachshund, Max, died," she said. "He was getting older and I should have seen it coming but I didn't. I've been so depressed ever since. I really miss him. I just haven't had the heart to get another dog to replace him. People keep telling me to move on but..." she stopped here and reached down, patting Lambkin's soft curls. She seemed lost in her own thoughts.

My final surprise involving this little lost dog came when KC looked at me and asked, "Would it be ok if I called my husband to see if we can keep Lambkins?"

Apparently, this matching of people and dogs (or dates) only works if you don't have a clue that you are doing it.

"Of course," I replied.

Was it possible that my two friends, one who called out to a stray dog and ended up with the animal in her lap and another who decided to

join me on a car ride and a drive-through lunch were the people God had chosen to provide a home for an abandoned dog? I held my breath as KC called her husband Scott and they talked. From the start of this adventure I hadn't thought of Lambkins as mine. It was clear however, that KC was in love. Her face was radiant as she talked to Scott and continued to pat the little dog in front of her. Finally she hung up and turned to me.

"Can we keep her? Scott says if I want her, it's ok with him." She looked at me hopefully.

Here was a friend who had lost a much loved pet two months before, a person who helped so many of us in her spare time with her generous spirit and great talent. Now, sitting in front of her, wagging its tail and jumping up with delight, was just what her heart needed. There was no question that this dog and owner were meant for each other. It there was such a thing as love at first sight between person and pet, I had just witnessed it.

"When should I bring her down?" I asked. We agreed that I would deliver Lambkins to them the following day, Friday.

When we returned to work from our lunch break, I was still a little stunned at what had happened. Many people told me how hard it was to get animals adopted so I didn't take what had just happened for granted. I knew in my heart it was no simple lunch date gone awry but rather a planned meeting of matched hearts.

Once I delivered Lambkins safely to their house, KC and Scott arranged for her to see a vet. They found out that she was about six years old and needed a fair amount of medical intervention to get in good shape. Her new parents lovingly provided her with what she needed and the dog began to blossom.

KC renamed Lambkins, "Toodles the Poodle," because she said, "I think she looks like a Toodles, don't you?" I guess a dog named Toodles is more likely to enjoy circus spinning than one named Lambkins so I agreed.

Now, every day when KC comes home from work, Toodles wants only one thing—to sit on KC's lap while she works on her art or relaxes for a few minutes. Apparently, when Toodles hears the garage door open and sees KC walk in, she jumps into KC's arms and vibrates for about ten minutes, shaking with delight at the sight of her new owner. I'm not sure I've ever had that kind of a reception at the end of a day.

As with all great loves, Toodles has some quirks that those who love her find endearing. During the day, she can be found sleeping in KC's closet in her laundry basket. Maybe she likes the soft bed of clothes. Maybe she just likes to feel near her new owner. When the basket is taken to the laundry room, Toodles goes to the closet and sleeps on KC's shoes. We may never know why, but we do know that when the day is over there is no baby gate or dog bed in the kitchen. Toodles simply climbs into bed with her new owners and snuggles up.

A few weeks after Toodles went to live with KC, I received an email from KC that said:

"Thanks for being so willing to help us with Toodles. You know, like you said, everything happens for a reason and I'm certain that's true, even more now than I believed it in the past. I've been struggling in my walk with God lately and I know you were thrown in my path for that reason. I know God is trying to get me back and you might be the step that gets me there again. Toodles is a little angel sent to remind me of what's most important in life and getting back to the basics of what it's all about. Let's go to lunch again so we can talk some more, k? When is a good day for you?"

KC

Toodles' appearance on my street had never been about me despite my worries and the claims of well-intentioned friends. She found a new life and even though she had jumped into my car, she landed in KC's heart. It may seem a common everyday occurrence to you, but I know better. Thanks to Toodles, I've finally witnessed what I've heard about for years but rarely seen first-hand —a match made in heaven.

THE BATTLE IS THE LORD'S

I heard his voice before I actually saw him. His laugh echoed through the room. There were happy greetings and audible pats on the back between him and my other friends in the front room. Then he came around the corner. His was a face I'd seen hundreds of times before. He had grown a beard and was wearing a baseball cap but I'd have known him anywhere. I'd forgotten how blue his eyes were and his smile reminded me of happy times. We'd spent many years during our twenties playing music together, singing about what God was doing in our lives.

It is great to hug an old friend and know that you can pick up right where you left off with him, no matter how much time has passed. There was a kind of love deposit left in our group of friends from those long ago days. We had deposited our youthful hearts into each other and the passing of time only seemed to increase the value of the accounts we had opened. It was a defense against lean times and it never seemed to diminish.

The last time I saw Tom he was traveling through Atlanta on a business trip. We had dinner and talked old and new times. His schedule was busy but his business was doing well. Then, a few years later, I heard from him again. Pursued by the "Hound of Heaven" Tom decided to follow his heart and his God. After a surgery for back trouble, he spent two years doing volunteer work with a homeless shelter. Eventually he was drawn into full time ministry for those who had lost everything in life. For seven years he and his wife poured out their lives into God's homeless children as directors of a wonderful place called The Source.

"Before I started doing this, I don't think I ever even looked at a homeless person. They were simply something to avoid on the street. Now I can't think of anything else," he told me that day.

It was a far cry from his years as a corporate whiz kid, the golden boy of opportunity.

Tom's years in business reminded me of an old family story about my cousin, Andy. When Andy was in kindergarten, his teacher asked each of the children to draw a picture of himself. My cousin thought for a minute, applied crayon to paper and handed it to his teacher.

Taking the picture from him, she glanced at it and frowned.

"Andy, this is a picture of a car," she commented patiently. "I asked you to draw a picture of yourself."

"I know it's a car but I'm in it," he replied, a little put out with her lack of vision.

Looking more closely at the drawing she wrinkled her forehead and squinted, trying hard to find anything resembling a little boy in the crayon drawing. She only saw four wheels, the body of a car, and two windows, a side view of the vehicle. Try as she might, she couldn't find Andy in the picture.

"I don't see any people in the picture," she said, glancing at Andy with a puzzled look on her face.

Andy puffed his cheeks out and released his breath in a long sigh. With all the dignity he could muster, he looked at his teacher and stated the obvious. "That's because the car is going so fast you can't see me!"

Like my young cousin's car, Tommy's life in corporate America had been traveling at high speeds. Eventually, the person driving it had almost vanished. Then, he found the homeless mission.

My friends and I all moved out onto the porch, feeling the warmth of the sun and the light Florida breeze brush our faces. There was so much to talk about. We'd heard through Tommy's latest newsletter that he and his Board of Directors had purchased a tract of land as a next step for folks who were making progress and getting their lives back together at the homeless center. Here they would build a center to help people learn additional "life skills" such as how to handle money, get a job, and manage the stress of everyday life. Eventually it would accommodate inexpensive housing for those ready to take the next step back into life.

Unexpectedly, a group of neighbors who lived adjacent to the land Tommy had bought, decided they did not want it used to make houses for rebuilt lives. The next thing you know there were injunctions and court battles and all kinds of confusion surrounding the effort to provide a new start for them.

This was a battle Tommy had not seen coming. After all, the land was previously the home of an alcohol rehabilitation center. Why would their potential neighbors be upset with its newly intended use? Maybe they considered permanent living amongst the previously homeless a step down from temporary housing for those with alcohol problems. The town council had verbally agreed when Tom's group purchased the land that it would remain zoned for its intended use. Once the neighbors began their complaining, every one of the council members backed away from their promises and left Tom to deal with the issue on his own.

After months of legal sparring, both groups finally ended up in court. Legions of people were praying for Tom and his team and, I imagine, just as many people were praying to block him. We had no idea how Tom could win this battle, for his opposition had lots of money to spare as well as friends in high places. Life in a small Florida town can apparently turn on you in a moment.

The day of the hearing finally arrived. Tom and his lawyer showed up in the small courtroom and sat down. Across from them was a table filled with lawyers representing the "no build" neighbors. The hearing began and both sides were given the chance to state their cases. It didn't take long for Tommy to see that things were not going well for his side. The highly paid lawyers for the opposition, and there were several of them present, had done a thorough job of explaining why the land Tom's team had purchased should be re-zoned to exclude using it for its promised purpose. The more these lawyers talked, the less his lawyer had to say. Tom sensed that any minute the hearing would be over and he would be left holding the property with no hope of it helping those he so cared about.

Unable to contain himself any longer and sure that his lawyer considered the case all but over, Tom determined to stand up and speak.

"I've got to say something!" he thought. "Someone has got to say something to persuade this judge that we have a contract and rights to this property!"

Just as he was rising to speak, he felt a tug in his heart. A scripture flashed through his mind.

"Be still and know that I am God." (Psalm 46:10) Tommy recognized the verse and it stopped him in his tracks. A peace settled over him. He stopped, closed his mouth and sat back down without speaking. Then he watched in wonder as something unusual happened.

Almost immediately the topic of "jurisdiction" arose. The lawyers for the prosecution began to argue amongst themselves about whether this particular court had jurisdiction over the issue at hand. Confusion followed as lawyers, who were all supposed to be working for his opposition, spoke openly against each other and the court. As they continued squabbling in front of the judge and the observers, they convinced themselves that the issue of how to use this land could not be decided in the current court and that it would have to be moved to another venue. The judge agreed. With a crack of his gavel, the judge closed the hearing, moving it to another time and place deemed more appropriate.

Tommy was stunned. What had just happened? Confusion had reigned in the opposing camp and the tide had turned in favor of the homeless. Tom hadn't had to say a word, he'd simply "been still."

My friend had spent the past several months doing what he felt God wanted him to do. He had bought the land and responded to the charges and found a lawyer to represent the cause of the homeless. He had talked to the powerful and cajoled the town council. But in the end, those who fought him found themselves fighting not Tom, but the goodness of God. It wasn't Tom's battle, it was the Lord's. And Tommy, who was to continue to lead this battle and this group of rag tag soldiers for several years to come, learned that there is a leader who knows every detail, every move and every tactic of the enemy. Tommy may have been the general, but there was a Chief above him to guide his effort to places he himself could not see. Sometimes all that is required is to "be still."

That's very counterintuitive you know. Being still doesn't come easy to any of us. If you've ever had an illness or injury that has taken you out of circulation for a while or felt that your efforts were especially ineffective, you know this. We feel that all forward motion comes from us, from the energy that we expend to put things in motion and keep them there. Apparently that is not always true. Apparently what is even more important is to follow the One who created all forward motion and energy in the very beginning.

To this date, I don't know if anything has been resolved for Tommy and his group concerning how the land can be used. What I do know is what his face reflected on the day he told me this story. It reflected the wonder of seeing what a loving God can do when you let Him. God participates in the moments of our lives, sometimes in the most unexpected ways. He knows what we need and if we are willing to let Him work and listen and respond to His still small voice, we get a front seat in the theatre of God's presence in this life.

I have one final thought on all this. In the book The Shack,[6] two of the main characters, Mack and Jesus, discuss whether people live their lives in the past, present, or future. The discussion leads to the realization that Mack, like many of us, spends most of his time in the past or future, reliving what he can't change or trying to control what he can't yet see. Mack, like us, often ignores the present moment and by missing it, he misses today's miracle.

Tommy could have missed the miracle too. He could have been so worried about what he had forgotten to do yesterday to help win the case that he missed the message to "be still." He could have been living in the fear of what awaited him if he returned to his group and told them they had lost the case. Instead, he managed to live in the moment with God, hearing a whisper of hope in his heart that asked him to let God join him in that moment. And because he did, he witnessed not only the ability of God to help us in our now, but also His desire to be a part in all we do.

CHAPTER 5

THE FIFTH PROMISE OF HOPE:
HE IS IN THE INCOMPLETE PARTS

Hope grows when we recognize Him in the incomplete Parts of our lives.
Hope helps us to recognize God in the incomplete and tells us that we don't have to know the end of the story to see Him in today.

"I remember my affliction and my wandering, the bitterness and the gall. I well remember them and my soul is downcast within me. Yet this I call to mind and therefore I have hope. Because of the Lord's great love we are not consumed, for his compassions never fail. They are new every morning, great is your faithfulness. I say to myself, the Lord is my portion. Therefore I will wait for him. The Lord is good to those whose hope is in him."

Lamentations 3:19-25

THE BEAUTY OF A MOMENT

I heard the music and reached across the table to pick up the phone. I love the technology that allows a song to announce my phone calls, especially when they are from friends and family. Glancing at the display I saw my son Josh was calling. He is currently living in another state and, because I don't see him often, I especially look forward to hearing from him.

Josh has a passion for people and it shows. He thrives in jobs where he can find the most interaction with others. While he is working, he prays for the people he comes in contact with—whether they are coworkers or customers. During our call that day, he shared a story of a recent encounter with a woman at work.

For several weeks Josh had noticed that a female co-worker seemed particularly unhappy and he prayed that an opportunity to talk to her would open up. A few days earlier it had finally happened. She approached him on a break and began to share that she was deeply depressed, to the point of not wanting to live any more. Something had happened with her son and she felt little hope for the future. She just couldn't shake the feeling none of it was worth fighting for. Josh, who has been through his own dark valleys, could immediately relate to her. After he listened to her story, he shared his own experience with depression. It occurred to him it might also help his new friend if she could speak with another woman who had been through a similar situation. On a whim, he picked up the phone and called a friend, a missionary who worked in the Bahamas, whom he hoped was in town that day. She was and readily agreed to join them for a meal.

It was one of those moments that seemed orchestrated to happen; an answer to prayer with just the right ingredients available—time to talk, a person who "happened" to be in town who could relate to this woman and her struggles, and a coworker who cared enough to pray and knew of resources to help. There were tears and sharing and a moment in time when there was a crack in a troubled everyday existence. That crack allowed some light to come in. My son was thrilled to be a part of the experience.

I asked him, "What happened in the end?"

"As we were leaving, we invited her to join us at our Wednesday night Bible Study/recovery group," he said. I knew he had found roots in those meetings and the kind of community and acceptance that encouraged him to keep growing. I was sure he hoped that his new friend would find the same. Then he wondered out loud if she would follow through, if she would take the next steps to find some lasting freedom and relief in her life.

His story made me think. I had experienced something recently that, although nothing like Josh's experience, seemed to relate to the question of 'what next?' In Josh's case, the question was whether the help received by his co-worker would be enough, whether this woman would follow through and whether this would become a defining moment in her life or just another day when she felt momentary relief from her deep struggles.

I have a plant called a Night Blooming Cereus. It's a very unusual plant that I'm pretty sure you can't buy at your local gardening store. As a matter of fact, I received mine as a Christmas present from a friend who had taken a cutting from her mother's plant, passed down to her through the generations. The plant itself is rather inglorious. It is ungainly and awkward looking and originally from dry, desert like territory. I think it's a type of cactus and it grows a flower that blooms once a year in a single night. That's right. From start to finish you can watch the beautiful bud that hangs from the rough "leaf" begin and end its blooming in a single night each year. If you have several buds, they all open together, as if orchestrated by a bloom choir director, each in perfect rhythm with the other.

It is an amazing thing to watch. When I realized this year that the bulb was ready to blossom I called several of my friends and said, "Hey, want to come over and watch a flower bloom tonight?" Despite the unusual request, over they came with flashlights and cameras to see for themselves. My daughter Jessica suggested throwing a party to watch a flower bloom might reflect something about my age. I swear this has nothing to do with getting older. It is an amazing event and worthy of an audience and a few hours of your time.

Shortly after the sun goes down and the darkness settles over the late summer landscape the bloom, completely closed and hanging from the side of the plant, begins to shake ever so slightly. As you watch, the tip opens just the tiniest bit. The process has begun. Over a period of about three hours it opens completely, from time to time shaking itself awake as it changes form in front of your eyes. I think the shaking has to do with the enormous amount of energy it is using to create the beautiful show in front of you.

It also emits an aroma every once in a while, mostly as it reaches its fully open state. The perfume wafting out is enchanting. The open blossom itself is intricately woven with fine threads in perfect rows creating a pattern at the bottom some call "the baby in the manger." At the end of the manger, a beautiful star shape unfolds.

As Josh talked about what might happen next for his friend, I began to think about how God creates. Like a flower blooming at night when few will see, He creates moments of hope for us that we sometimes miss. God doesn't spend His time just on things that have the highest chance of succeeding or being seen. He never looks at one of us and says, "I don't think Jan is going to get the message this time so call off the show! Don't bother to send someone over with a kind word or a much needed resource or a prayer. She's not listening."

No, instead, for each of us, He seems happy to pour over us just the balm we need whether or not we acknowledge or accept its healing power. Over and over I have seen for myself and heard stories from others about how they received something unusual and good but, not ready to move on, they took a quick look at a blessing from God and immediately forgot what they had been given.

For instance, the other night I heard a young woman tell her story at a Rainbow Village graduation. Rainbow Village is a place where homeless moms and children can go to rebuild their lives in a year-long program. Before Rainbow Village, this young woman was living in a relationship with an abusive man whom she finally left shortly before she gave birth to their child. Within a few months she decided to move back in with him. When she did her mother told her three things, "It will only get worse, you will end up having another child with this man, and you will lose everything." Despite the warning the young woman returned to the relationship.

Within a few months the abuse had escalated and she was pregnant again, this time with no insurance. She and her boyfriend moved from hotel to hotel to find a place to sleep each week. One day, when she was about five months pregnant and ill, her mother came to pick her and her child up for the day. While she was with her mother, she decided to leave her situation and move into a shelter for victims of domestic violence. Within a week she had been to the doctor and found out she was pregnant with twins. But her story was far from over. After finding and being accepted into Rainbow Village, she was given the time and resources to rebuild her life.

She admitted that she hadn't been ready to change until that day her mother came to get her. That was when she had truly reached the end of her rope. Still, all through her story as she revealed it, there were moments when God had met her right at her point of need, even when she could not yet take hold of the new life He was leading her toward.

God is a creator. He puts His very best into every moment, whether it is a flower that puts on an amazing show once a year, an abused woman escaping to new hope, or a depressed woman getting help from a coworker and his friend. He uses every willing resource available and He gives completely to the moment at hand. He does not give less when He knows the gift will be put aside. He creates in each day, in each life, the best for us no matter whether we recognize or appreciate it. The last time I heard, the sun still rises in an amazing show of light every morning whether we sleep through it or not.

My question to Josh about what happened at the end of his remarkable encounter with his coworker caused us both to wonder if the time spent with the woman in need would end up being time well spent. Would it reap a lifetime of healing or simply a moment of relief? But that wasn't really the point. The point was that God, in His infinite role as loving Creator, was willing to create a moment of beauty for a troubled heart. I'm sure He desires for her to move toward Him on a more permanent basis and live in His grace. But whether this was her final step or simply one movement toward Him, He will be there when she reaches out again.

A God who cares enough to pour his energy into a plant that unfolds in an incredible display in a single night once a year is a God who loves beauty in every form. Maybe Josh's coworker's beauty is just beginning to unfold. Maybe, like the Rainbow Village mother, she will need more time, light and nourishment before she can move into true freedom. For that day, God was happy to create a landscape of love just for her, a moment of blooming with the sweet fragrance of His love lingering, even if only for an evening.

God is the God of every moment, whether we recognize His works or not. Don't let the moment pass you by.

CAUTION: MAY CAUSE DIZZINESS

Recently I woke up with a case of vertigo. That means when you glance over at your bedside clock early in the morning to see if it's time to get up, the world starts to spin. After that, almost every time you look up, down or just about anywhere but straight ahead for the next some unknown amount of time, the exact same thing happens. It's not the kind of fun spinning like on a ride at Six Flags, it's more like the kind you had when you were sixteen, had too much to drink for the first time ever, and lay down on a bed that immediately began to spin out of control. For those who were smart enough not to try the last behavior but would still like to truly empathize with the vertigo sufferer, try hanging upside down for an hour, then turn around in fast circles, and immediately eat some pizza. Basically this condition just makes you want to throw up.

Obviously, I decided rather quickly this was something I wanted to get resolved. Being new to the world of unexpected spinning, except for that time in high school where I was in my experimenting phase, I decided that my chiropractor could help. I thought maybe it was a problem with my neck and its alignment. After all, alignment in life and spine are not easily maintained. The chiropractor, Dr. Mayfield, listened to my problem and immediately sent me in to see the MD who works with him to make sure my symptoms weren't a reflection of something more sinister. She told me in no uncertain terms I had "benign positional vertigo." Benign is a word welcomed in every medical setting I can imagine. It didn't feel very benign but apparently, according to the doctor, it had no deadly intentions toward me.

She gave me some medicine and sent me home. I should have known when the pharmacist said, "This medicine may make you a little dizzy," that something was up. Two days later things hadn't improved, so I went to my primary care physician. He gave me the same diagnosis and a "patch" to wear behind my ear that apparently is very helpful for people who are prone to seasickness. Looking at the instructions before I stuck the thing behind my ear, I was surprised to read "May cause dizziness." After all, it's Dramamine. That stuff will put you to sleep in a hurricane!

A week later, the spinning was still on track so I ended up at the Ear, Nose and Throat specialist. He did a very cool move with my head and told me to sleep sitting up for two nights so his healing maneuver could settle in my inner ear. I did it but almost fell off the chair during the night and I'm pretty sure my head flopped over to the side a fair amount—a sure recipe for continuing to feel off balance. Finally the spinning from the vertigo went away but not the dizziness.

Back to the specialist I went. He wanted me to wait a month or two to see if I healed on my own but I practically begged him to think harder and see if there was anything else that might be impacting all this. Two weeks had passed and the holidays were upon us. I was longing to get on a plane and go see my daughter for Thanksgiving and I needed help! After chatting for a bit longer, he decided I might also be experiencing a recalcitrant Eustachian tube acting up in tandem with the vertigo. He gave me a steroid to address it. I went to a different drug store on my way home because I was getting a little self-conscious about all the visits. I mean, I like my pharmacist just fine, but I wasn't used to seeing him quite this often and I didn't want to earn some kind of "frequent flyer" status at the drug store.

When the new clerk handed me my package twenty minutes later, he said innocently, "Do you have any questions for the pharmacist?" "No!" I said, afraid of what I might hear about this particular cure. I sped away in my car as quickly as possible not wanting to know if my new prescription was also a dizzy or drowsy medical intervention. Finally my curiosity got the better of me and I gave in, reading the entire dire list of potential side effects. Sure enough, there it was— "dizziness."

After another episode of vertigo occurred a few weeks later, I realized that these things can be tough to tame. Apparently the microscopic crystals residing in your inner ear, when moved around by mysterious forces, can wreak havoc on you. The good news is that after a few more visits to an additional super-duper specialist, I'm still dizzy but no longer spinning. Call me crazy but I consider the lack of spinning to be a huge improvement in my condition. So what if I'm perpetually off balance and people seem fuzzier than normal? Apparently after taking all this medicine and waiting three weeks to three months, I should be good as new. (See **Living Between the Promise and the Command** for more.)

But you have to admit that all this is a little ironic, as well as annoying and potentially indicative of the fact that I expect all diseases to be fixed fast, without all this time and medicine involved. For those of you who are busy judging me for running up the cost of health care all over America with my doctor visits and medicine binge, I suggest you try walking around upside down for a few days and then you can come back to me with advice. By the way, don't send me your homemade remedies. I tried to eat a ginger root in the middle of all this at the advice of someone I love dearly, and I almost burned my taste buds raw.

The question is, why in the world would a medicine, or medicines, with the potential side effect of producing the very thing you are trying to get rid of, be the thing that fixes you? Is all medicine dizzy inducing? I know life induces dizziness, but medicine too? Or is it just that once you are off balance for a while, everything in your life follows suit and starts leaning to one side as well?

I know there is a spiritual parallel in all this—it's seems like just the kind of thing I experience in my relationship with God. The very thing I would avoid, God suggests I should do to help resolve my spiritual ills. In the Bible, Jesus often prescribes what I call "upside down" remedies for our brokenness. If you follow His dosing directions, it is like taking a hope potion for what ails you. You always get better if you stick with the medicine.

For instance, when you are faced with someone you just can't stand, instead of giving them a piece of your mind and setting them straight once and for all, which seems to be the obvious treatment, Jesus prescribes loving them. He is pretty clear about forgiving and loving our enemies. He even expands on the thought with the idea that you need to heap "coals of kindness" on these obnoxious folks. That is some intense kindness, not a quick prayer and some well wishes. Nothing less than actions filled with His love will suffice.

He tells us to give first, not expect others to give to us first. *"Give and it will be given to you. A good measure, pressed down, shaken together and running over, will be poured into your lap. For with the measure you use, it will be measured to you."* Luke 6:38 NIV

Wow. So I should offer to help others at work before I ask them to help me? Or, in traffic, I should let someone else in line in front of me instead of assuming people who don't move over for me are complete jerks? By the way, this is a little off topic but I just found out that I live in the city that is number three in the nation in road rage. That explains a lot of my trials and tribulations.

Here's an interesting one for you. Jesus tells us not to judge, unless we want to be judged and then, in another part of the New Testament, St. Paul says "The person with the Spirit makes judgments about all things."(1 Corinthians 2:15, NIV) I don't want to make you dizzy or anything, but it sounds like we aren't supposed to condemn others while we are expected to "judge" or discern the truth about situations with the wisdom He gives us. Still, it's a little tricky the first time you read it.

How about this one? You can't work your way to heaven. I know you work your way up the ladder at your job, you work at home or school and you work on your relationships—or at least I hope you do. This is good, you are supposed to work but you can't work your way to God. Instead, He worked His way to us, became one of us, and paved the way back to God. For you self-starters, type A's and 'I can do it by myself' kind of folks, this may be disturbing news. It's not your goodness that gets you to God, its God goodness that gets you to Him. Feeling off balance yet? Or is the medicine starting to take effect?

If you are beginning to understand that God's love, vast and dizzying in its greatness, forgives us when we act like His enemies, guides us so we can judge correctly in order to follow Him closer, and came first to us before we thought of coming to Him, then the prescription is working. Even if you are still feeling the effects of your wobbly life, hold on. It takes time but if you let Him, He removes the leftover effects of your old life and replaces your brokenness, one piece at a time, with wholeness. If you are left lightheaded by all this good news, concerned about the side effects of His love, don't worry.

He'll take care of the vertigo and you can trust Him with the leftover dizziness. At least that's what I'm hoping for.

TWISTER

Sometime in the middle of the night I dreamt that there was a tornado right outside my back door. This wasn't the kind of tornado you see from a distance, reaching down from the heavens like a dragon gone mad, slashing the earth with its twisting tail. This one was so close you couldn't see its form at all, only a dark, leaden gray mass filling the door frame. It was like the scene in the Wizard of Oz when Dorothy sat on her bed in Auntie Em and Uncle Henry's flying house as the storm winds carried the world and its debris by her. However, unlike Dorothy's storm scene, nothing was flying by my door; everything was completely still. I was reminded of another movie, Twister, where those who dared chase the storm stood in the path of something so large that it swallowed houses as easily as eighteen wheelers and cows. The scene felt familiar. What I was witnessing was massive and I hadn't even seen it coming until it had already filled my doorway. By the way, I only had a screen door between myself and that monster.

That's how it goes some days. You only get a split second before the tornado that is filling your back yard actually hits your house and there is nothing but thin mesh wire to blunt its impact. Often it all feels like a dream until you realize you are already awake. I think that may be how Alice was feeling when she thought back to her story.

I was just now learning what happened to her five years before. All this time I'd never had a clue that anything was wrong. It's funny, because I saw her almost every day in the break room where we worked. She always had a smile on her face and I never heard an unhappy word from her. I remember when she was having a lot of back pain and even then I don't remember her complaining. She just explained to me what was happening and how she was trying to deal with it. Anyone who has ever had lingering back pain knows it's next to impossible not to grumble about it at least a little bit. If she did, I don't recall it. That's how I see Alice; dealing with her pain and getting on with her life, practical and upbeat.

Alice is a thirty something woman who works in one of our technical groups. She is slender and short, with a pretty, oval face and expressive eyes. I first met her in the classroom at work where I it was easy to see that she was an avid learner. After taking several classes on a variety of topics, she decided she wanted to grow her leader skills. That meant she had to apply for our company's Leader Certification Program which entailed having a current development plan, direct reports and approval from her leader to be eligible to participate. Most people finished the program in about a year but with the heavy schedules many were experiencing, we gave them additional time if they needed it. Alice was immediately accepted into the program.

When she came to speak to me that day, almost five years later, I knew little of how our training program had impacted her day to day work. In hindsight I should have checked up on her. We worked in different areas of the company and I simply assumed, in the absence of feedback, that all had gone well. That is, until she approached me and told me she wanted to share something with me. She said she hadn't talked to anyone about what happened all those years ago. She was too embarrassed at the time to tell me.

As it turned out, the day after she had graduated from our leader program, the day after her boss had attended our graduation lunch, the day after she had passed the tests and shared an example of a successful leader experience with those gathered for the celebration, she had been demoted. When she told me this, she looked stricken. I didn't know what to say. It was clear something had gone terribly wrong and it was way too late for me to try to make things right. She indicated that she was 'over it' but if that was true, why was she informing me about it now? When I asked her she said, "I just felt like I should tell you."

So I asked her to meet with me at another time and share the whole story. Maybe together we could make some sense of it.

A week or so later we sat together in a small restaurant on a rainy afternoon, Alice across from me in the booth looking a little uncomfortable. I was starting to focus in earnest on this book and was hoping that maybe her story would be one I could share with others. From what she had told me the previous week, she had found meaning in what happened to her though it had at first eluded her. I kept thinking about Joseph, a Biblical character who had his life hijacked by his brothers. Years later when they finally came to him for help and forgiveness he said to them, *"you meant evil against me, but God meant it for good in order to bring about [a]this present result."* (Genesis 50:20a NASB) I sensed this was a theme in Alice's story as well.

As she went back over the details of her sudden demotion on the heels of her graduation from our leader program, it occurred to me that her story wasn't completely unfamiliar. Managers at every level of every company, like parents and teachers and politicians, are all destined to fall short of the expectations of their constituency. I think it is built into the contract somewhere. Whether they mean to or not, they can and do mishandle situations involving their people. Alice felt sure her manager had.

It was the shock factor that made her story so impactful. Her leader asked her to join him in a meeting the day after her graduation and she'd had no idea why. Once there, he told her that the company wanted to reduce some layers of management and would no longer need her services as a manager. There would be no change in her pay and there were no performance complaints. There were no previous warnings of poor performance and no such objections arose at that time. According to her manager, this had nothing to do with her personally other than the fact that she was a leader and there were one too many leaders in their group.

Alice was completely blindsided. She had not seen this coming at all. Her career train had appeared to be going at full speed in one direction and then suddenly it had been derailed. Not only did it stop its forward motion, there was a fair amount of carnage lying by the tracks when it was all over. The biggest casualty was Alice's self-esteem and her trust. Months of questioning her own worth followed her leader's announcement, which had been delivered as unemotionally as if he had been sharing a recipe or a phone number. She also spent a fair amount of time questioning him and his motives. I was sorry to hear that she had been ashamed and embarrassed by the event, for that had kept her from talking about it. Instead of reaching out, she had gone home and curled up in her bed, longing to escape.

When she returned to work she didn't try to change the outcome by talking her leader or their department head into changing their minds.

"I realized the deal was done, the papers signed, and I had no advocate. My leader had already been given the authority to do what he had done," she said.

Instead Alice went into a shell. She stopped socializing, especially with those who had previously been her direct reports. There had been no meeting with the team to explain her leader's actions and her new role. She didn't know how they had found out what had happened, only that they had been informed without her being present. She had no idea what her direct reports thought, but she assumed they would believe that somehow it was a reflection on her.

"They knew I had been demoted and I felt they were all talking about me. I thought everyone knew so I tried to stay at my desk. I couldn't face what I assumed they were thinking—that there was something wrong with my performance and I just wasn't good enough."

She stopped taking classes and who could blame her? Previously a high performer, she stopped going the extra mile and offering to work overtime. Even after finally telling another person outside her department what had happened to her, she did nothing. Her fear told her that stirring the waters would only lead to something worse and, as a single female, she could not afford to lose her job. Standing between her and action were too many bills to pay and too little experience with other companies to understand her real worth.

What struck me most in her story was that she told no one. But then, Alice wasn't a complainer, remember? Only this time, what she was carrying inside needed to be said and as long as it remained hidden, it continued to erode her self-esteem, slowing her heart with the weight of her anger and insecurity. I wished the anger had won this battle. I wished she had reached out and kept reaching out until one of us finally had to look into the matter and give her what she deserved—either better treatment or an apology for something badly mishandled.

What she hadn't counted on was the strength of her faith. As she fought to surface for breath from the pool of this seeming injustice, she found herself turning to her heavenly Father.

"I finally prayed about it," she told me that day. "It gave me courage to go back to work and hold my head up. It also gave me the courage to decide I should be treated better. I told myself that I needed a job and benefits at that time but that I would eventually leave this company. Until I started praying, I had been upset with God as well as with my boss. I'm kind of a sensitive person," she said, lowering her head slightly and averting her eyes.

I know what it's like to take things too much to heart. It had taken me years to realize that some arrows aimed at me were really just the by-product of someone else's pain or ignorance. I hoped that someday she would realize her sensitivity could be a source of great strength and not simply an indication of weakness.

"I felt I had done everything right and still gotten this unfair treatment. Was this part of God's plan for me? If so, it was really painful and I had already suffered significant rejection in my childhood. This just felt like one more rejection. One night while praying I had the thought that I should quit worrying and let my anger go. I felt I needed to give it all to God to figure out," Alice told me.

So she did, telling Him that night, "I will leave it all to you—all my emotions and feelings—and I will keep my peace."

Like many moments in our lives that are so profound and have such lasting impact, it seemed so simple. This became the turning point for Alice.

"I can be really stubborn," she told me, "but after this, hope began to grow back in my heart. Instead of turning in a letter of resignation I decided I would not walk away from my job until I was ready. I began to pray and ask God what was next." Her words were coming out more powerfully now and I could feel the passion of them wash over her again as she recalled her new resolve.

"I decided this would be my last job working for someone else and I began taking courses and researching opportunities at the small business administration. At the time I knew nothing besides technology and I needed to figure out what I wanted to do next." She paused and then began again. "One day I was driving down the highway and it popped into my head. I suddenly knew what my passion was."

When I asked her to tell me more, she said she wasn't ready. She didn't want to talk to others about her new plan until she could actually put it into place. I guess you need to give some things room to grow before you expose them to too many outsiders.

Through all this, Alice had not only identified her new passion but had also determined to continue in her current job until she had saved enough money to pursue her new direction. That day on the highway, when she realized what she really wanted to do with the rest of her life, her excitement began to erase her sense of loss. She no longer thought about her demotion and instead began focusing on her future.

"I used to ask the question, 'Why'," she said. " 'Why was I demoted? Why did it happen that way?' Eventually I realized that it was to get me to this very point, the point where I realize if I don't like a path, I can start over. If there hadn't been any pain where I was, I might have become complacent and never ventured out. As a result of what happened to me, I now have a plan in place, a proposed timeline based on the economy and my financial position, and even a mentor who is already doing what I love and is happy to take me under her wing."

At this point in our conversation I could see Alice's natural peace radiating again. She'd relived the emotions of that hard time in her life while sharing it with me and it had been a strain on her. But in showing me her pain and rejection, she found some additional relief. It is hard to witness those parts of peoples' hearts that have been so badly bruised. When I am the one witnessing the pain, I worry that I won't have the right words to say. I forget a truth I learned years ago--that sometimes just to share a hurt with another caring heart is to be relieved of it. No other action is required of the listener than to hear and accept.

Alice was wrapping up now. *"And we know that in all things God works for the good of those who love him, who have been called according to His purpose."* (Romans 8:28, NIV) she quoted to me from Romans. "I think I have grown through all this and one of the good things that has come from it is that I no longer look for the promotion and applause of other people. I pat myself on my back and chart my own course, with God leading the way. I've learned that my career is in my hands and I can trust God to keep my hand in His. I don't need to be immobilized by fear and disappointment."

Then Alice, in one more moment of vulnerability, asked me a question.

"What is it about me that I have to deal with this spirit of rejection over and over?"

I'd felt during our conversation that there was more to all this than just a story of events past, that maybe there was a need for additional healing. Alice had received part of what God wanted to give her but one thing was left over from what happened. She was partially motivated to change so that others could no longer reject her. My experiences had taught me that fear of rejection can be as powerful a master as a boss who just doesn't get it. Real freedom for Alice didn't lie in never being open to others again, in being protected from the possibility of rejection. Real freedom lay in the healing of the heart so that those rejections lost their sting. Fear is a misleading master and will lead you away from your true calling as surely as complacency.

We sat in that restaurant and with Alice's permission I prayed for her right there. The rain washed against the outside of the building as we asked God to send healing waters to wash over her heart.

When I had first agreed to listen to Alice I told her that maybe I could take what she told me and share it in my book. It now appeared that we had gotten together for much more than that. We had met for more healing—the kind that comes when you take another person's hand in yours and together turn to a God who rejects no one who calls on Him. We held on to each other and we held on to Him as we asked Him to set Alice free to pursue with a new heart all that is before her.

You see, in the end, no story is just a story. It is a moving of hearts from one place to another and every story is still being written, even when we think we've learned all we can from it. Even after five years. Even after heartbreak and healing. Even when it's your story.

CHAPTER 6

THE SIXTH PROMISE OF HOPE:
HOPE GROWS IN PATIENCE

Hope grows in Patience.

Hope tells us to be patient, that God hears our prayers even when he chooses to answer them over time.

"But hope that is seen is no hope at all. Who hopes for what he already has? [25]But if we hope for what we do not yet have, we wait for it patiently."

Romans 8:24-25

THE WAITING ZONE

A rousing presentation at the Sales Conference started it all. Somewhere between the new products discussion and the Q&A, a little snowball of an idea entered my head and took on a life of its own. I quickly realized that to bring my idea to life, I would need some help. Looking around the room I thought I saw just the right person; Damian. His job involved both videotaping and editing and I was hoping he could spare a few minutes to help me get our associates interested in some new learning opportunities.

I'm in the business of learning in corporate America. Luckily, during this time in my career I worked for a company whose business was cable, web, and mobile media. Videotaping was a part of our company's core skill set. That meant that my idea—a series of short, fun, learning videos to teach associates about company basics-- was within the realm of possibility. I was hoping that Damian could help me translate my concept into reality, or at least point me to someone who could.

It was break time and I realized that our sales associates had headed out of the conference room into the hallway, aiming straight toward a table covered with fresh fruit and bagels. I saw Damian in the crowd. Winding my way through the other conference attendees, I tapped him on the shoulder and asked if he had a moment. He smiled, nodding, and we moved away from the others so we could talk. I shared my latest idea with him and he assured me he would be happy to help. We talked for a few minutes more and then noticed everyone moving back toward the meeting room. As I turned to leave, Damian looked at me thoughtfully.

"Can I ask you a question 'off the record'?" he blurted out.

His face took on a worried look, his eyes full of something I couldn't name. Even though I was officially part of the Human Resources department, I was in the learning and development side of our business. So sometimes when an employee needed insight into company policy but they weren't sure they wanted to ask their question "officially," they approached me. I would try to provide some perspective on their issue and if they wanted to pursue it further, I sent them to the experts on our team who could give them concrete answers.

"Go ahead," I said, reminding him up front that if his topic had anything to do with an infringement of employment law, I would have to refer him immediately to an HR Director. He nodded understanding and we turned and started walking down the hall away from the rest of our group. Damian looked at me thoughtfully and began his story.

Our company had recently been sold, and in the process it had promised severance packages to those whose jobs were affected by the change in ownership. It turned out that Damian's position was one of the jobs being eliminated. His manager, however, had offered to transfer him to another position—one that he did not want to take. The new job was on an evening shift, when Damian normally cared for his son, a special needs child. He felt that he could not take the job and continue to care for his son as before. Being asked to move from his current job to this new one created an uncomfortable predicament for Damian. Because the company was offering him an alternative to his current job, refusing the new position would leave him without work as well as make him ineligible for a severance package. It seemed a lose/lose proposition for him.

I was following the conversation pretty well, asking questions and interjecting advice as it seemed appropriate. Then he said something that surprised me. Damian told me that he had been working part time with a local church and was being mentored for a leadership position there. His heart was in the ministry, not in his current work. He was emotionally ready to leave our company but he really needed a financial cushion to get from where he was to where he wanted to go. He had just written a book targeted to college kids and young adults struggling with their faith in God. There were several other things in his life that indicated now was the time for him to move toward his new goal. Only money, or lack of it, seemed to stand in his way.

Call me slow, but I was just beginning to understand that Damian's and my little get together that day had very little to do with my video series and a whole lot to do with his current predicament. Damian wanted to step into the plan he felt God had for his life but was unsure of how to do that. He needed to bounce his thoughts off someone and I had shown up. You have to admit, leaving a permanent job when you have a full time special needs child to care for, even if you have a working spouse, seems very risky to say the least. I sensed that Damian was at a turning point in his life, wanting to move forward but needing some encouragement to do so.

During our conversation, it had become clear to me that Damian was a follower of Christ, something I hadn't realized before. For the second time that day, an unusual idea popped into my head.

"Damian, I need to ask you a question. I can't advise you on your scenario as an HR professional because I don't think your question is really about our company's policy or about employment law. So can we refocus away from the world of work for a moment into what we'll call 'God's World'? Can we look at your circumstances through the eyes of faith? I don't think we can have this conversation unless we bring Him front and center as we speak."

He lit up. "Yes, please!" he said.

We walked outside together and I began to tell Damian about a time in my life when I had to surrender everything in order to move forward. My son had been in a desperate place emotionally and physically for several years and at the time I wasn't sure if he would survive. It appeared to be a very real possibility that he wouldn't. One night during this time, I told Damian, I went to dinner with a neighbor of mine. She asked me how my son was doing.

"It's looking really bad," I said. "and I don't know what else to do to help."

I knew God was at work in our situation but my heart felt like it was swimming upstream, working overtime to find His presence in my family's crisis. I looked at my neighbor and knew that she too had things in her life that challenged her ability to see God and His goodness. Something in me didn't want to leave my friend and I both locked in our fear and hopelessness. Then I said something that surprised both of us.

"It looks bad," I said, "but…." I hesitated for a minute and it seemed in that moment that my mind was rushing to catch up with my heart. "But I trust God with my son. If I can't trust God with my son, I can't trust Him at all. Whether my son lives or dies, I trust God with him." As the words tumbled out, my heart shifted into a new gear.

I felt as if I had spoken something into being. It was as if the hope and faith that had been wrestling its way around my heart had finally made its way front and center. While it may not sound like much to you, that statement was at the center of a pivotal moment for me. I was declaring God's absolute sovereignty over my life and the life of my child and my absolute dependence on Him and His goodness, no matter what might happen.

My immediate thought was that I had just put God on the spot with my neighbor, who seemed to want to trust God too. Like me, she had her challenges. Now she would be a first hand witness to the results of my renewed reliance on God. I knew in that moment that either God would step in with a miracle for my family or I would trust him in our tragedy.

My second thought was that I had committed myself to no longer looking just to the immediate, observable results of my son's battle. Instead I began to focus on God, on His faithfulness and His knowledge of all things, even the meaning in disaster and loss. I had released my son to my heavenly Father, no matter what the consequences, no matter what the outcome. I was grateful that His Spirit had urged my heart's surrender that evening, because at the time I had been completely panicked, falling off the edge of my life with no rail to break the fall. Things shifted that day and I began to lean heavily into God. Trust has never been my strong point but now I was declaring my absolute reliance on Him. Life was taking me someplace new, a ship on stormy seas with faith as my only sail.

"Damian, while this is my story, it is playing out in another version for you. In your life, the situation with your job is similar to my circumstances with my son. It isn't working but you are holding on, rolling with the punches to help keep it alive while fearful of the results. Are you willing to trust God with your job, whether it lives or dies? Are you willing to take a leap in faith, ask God for what you need, and trust Him with the outcome? If you are, then refuse the new job and ask for your severance anyway. The risk is that you could put everything in jeopardy and end up with no job and no money to tide you over. However, if you accept the new position, you cannot meet the needs of your son or your own heart. Your role in all this is to trust God completely and follow what He is telling you. Say what needs to be said to our company leaders and let God handle the rest. "

Damian lit up—his face taking on a light that had been missing until now. "I'm going to call my wife today and see what she says and then I am going to ask for my severance instead of a job transfer!"

He was so excited and the energy of the Holy Spirit was so powerful that we both were caught up in the moment. It wasn't until later that day that I had time to reflect on what had happened.

"Oh Lord, I've just suggested to a child of Yours that he quit his job even if that leaves him without money to support his family! What in the world was I thinking?" I was glad that Damian had mentioned he was going to talk to his wife before he took my outrageous advice. I prayed that God continue to lead him in the direction He wanted.

Later that evening at a dinner following the sales conference, Damian got back to me. He and his wife were in joyful agreement about his next steps. He had immediately approached his HR Director with his proposition and the Director appeared to be very open to his request. Things were looking positive. Damian and his wife were sure that God would provide, that the tide had turned, and that His provision would come in. Certainly circumstances seemed to indicate that the events of this day would provide them what they wanted. God was at work!

About a month later I heard back from Damian again. After thirty days he still had no definitive answer regarding his refusal to transfer and his appeal for severance. Nothing. His unusual request had gone from his HR representative to those in the organization who could make the final decision. No answer had been forthcoming. Not a yes, not a no. Damian was still hopeful but he had begun wondering if he would soon be told there was no job and no severance for him after all. So much for our divinely inspired rendezvous a few weeks earlier!

Time went by and I wondered often if anything had happened. There was no word from Damian and I felt sure that he would call once something broke. What had at one time looked so promising was beginning to look less so every day. Did we misunderstand? Maybe it wasn't God who had been speaking in our hearts that day. Maybe it was wishful thinking.

I have since learned that all true God seekers find themselves at this place at some point in their lives. We start with a dream—a dream to use the gifts God has given us or to follow something in our hearts that speaks to us. We pray about it, we think about it, and we ask others what they think. Then the moment comes. Something that seems beyond coincidence occurs and we move toward our dream, sure in our faith and our God. Then, nothing. Time passes and nothing happens. There is no change in our circumstance. What looked like a decision made in faith stalls, adrift and without wind in stagnant waters.

Many people have described this place. Jeff Henderson at Buckhead Church in Atlanta did a series on it called the Waiting Room— comparing it to a visit to the doctor where you are trapped in the waiting room. While filling out endless forms, you wait impatiently for help to arrive, sure that your needs are greater than those of the other patients. Everyone else in the room is eventually called in to see the doctor but your turn never comes. Not even the nurse has any sympathy for you. When will you get the help you deserve?

I picture it like waiting at a bus stop. In my mind's eye I see several passengers sitting on a bench, a sign above their heads telling them this is where they board the bus. The sign above them says 'The Waiting Zone'. One person, a man headed to work, is sure that his bus will show up soon. After all, he checked the schedule in advance and he knows it is coming. He fully expects to get to his destination on time. He trusts the reliability of his city's public transportation system and has had good experience with it so far.

One bus comes but it is the downtown bus, headed in the opposite direction from where he wants to go. Several of his fellow passengers get on board. He continues to wait, crossing his legs in front of him and digging through his briefcase looking for something to read. Another bus drives by, but this one does not even pause at the Waiting Zone. It is not on his circuit. He begins to get restless, a worried look crossing his face.

Finally, after many buses have come and gone with the exception of the one he wants, he realized that he is the only one left on the bench. He puts away his book and it hits him that what he expected is not going to happen. At least not in the way he was hoping for. He thought he understood the system, understood the directions, understood what to do to get where he wanted to go. But it hasn't worked as he thought it would. He's seen other buses picking up passengers. He trusts that buses do indeed take people places all around the city. What about him? What should he do?

I have learned that this waiting and this hoping are irrevocably intertwined. My son shared with me recently that he had been reading scripture and came across a passage that was relevant to the topic of hope.

"But as for me, I watch in hope for the Lord, I wait for God my Savior; my God will hear me." Micah 7:7, NIV

After reading this scripture, Josh looked at the commentary on the page across from it and learned that the Hebrew word *yachal*, used in the previous passage, is interpreted interchangeably as either wait or hope. I was intrigued by his discovery. The more I thought about it the more sense it made. If we are waiting then we still do not have what we want. We will wait only as long as we hope. When we stop waiting it is because we have stopped hoping. We began to look at other scriptures referenced in his commentary and my son and I found passage after passage where this one word served two purposes in the same sentence.

For example Psalm 130 verses 5 and 7 declare *"I wait (yachal) for the Lord, my soul waits (yachal) and in his word I do hope (yachal.)"* In the very act of waiting you find the act of hoping.

This explains a lot. I already knew from my own personal experience that when I was patient and waited for God to come through that my hope in Him grew stronger. It was like working out my hope muscle and watching it strengthen. The expectation that something good is coming is what hope is all about and it often requires us to be patient and wait. If we give up hope too soon, we have much to lose. I just hadn't realized that the two concepts were so linked.

Damian, I was sure, was sitting on the bench in the Waiting Zone. After a few more months, I saw him again. He still had not heard what was going to happen to him at the company. This time when he spoke to me, I noticed he was almost serene about the absence of action. When I asked him why, he told me that he had surrendered his anxiety to God and in that surrender, his hope that God's hand was guiding the outcome of his situation had become sure. Instead of hoping for a specific result, his hope transformed into the knowledge, born of hope, that all was in God's hands and would work out for the best.

I can't say I was surprised when a few short weeks after that, Damian stopped by my office one afternoon.

"I'm leaving," he said with a smile.

"Did you get what you were hoping for?" I asked.

He nodded yes, excited with the knowledge that he would now be moving into full time ministry, working both at his church and with college students to help secure their faith in the One who had shown him how to wait and hope. I had learned two precious lessons from working with Damian—that hoping often requires us to wait and that we hope best when we hope in the person of God even more than in our desired result.

What can I say? Damian isn't the only one who is learning to wait and hope. I am hoping to finish this book. Maybe you are waiting on something as well. As it turns out, at least for me, it's not as hard as I thought once I realized who was driving the bus.

THE GOOSE CROSSING

Traffic was stopped. Not like it normally does when cars stop for traffic lights or when too many cars are on the road at once and there is nowhere else to go. No, there were two lanes of vehicles sitting mysteriously still in the middle of the road for no good reason that I could figure out. As I stretched my neck forward and turned my head to the side to take a closer look, I couldn't help but notice that the street was completely clear from the first inert vehicle at the front of the line all the way to the next traffic light. So, what was up?

That's when I saw it. Just at the bumper of the car in the front of the line, a small black beak appeared. It was followed immediately by a feathered head bobbing to the left and right as if its owner was slightly intoxicated. Another head appeared and then two more until I saw a squad of four Canadian geese waddling together across the street. I wondered if it was possible to get ticketed for "migrating under the influence."

The geese looked curiously at the line of autos, drawing a little closer together as new cars pulled up behind those who had already stopped. Their beautiful black and grey bodies looked slightly awkward rocking atop their big webbed feet. Maybe it was simply that I was more used to seeing geese fly than walk across the road. It appeared they were leaving the mall and heading over to a small parking lot fringed with trees and grass. Maybe the after-Christmas bargains weren't all that great and the geese had left the mall in search of something more fun. Whatever the reason, they certainly didn't appear to be up to date on proper use of crosswalks.

It is unexpected to find Canadian geese sauntering across a busy Atlanta roadway, curious but unconcerned with the metal giants humming so close to their sleekly feathered sides. But that wasn't what had surprised me most. What really surprised me about this scenario was that the cars had actually stopped. Not just one lane but two had completely halted to allow safe passage to the small entourage. We don't pause for much here in Atlanta, not even when we know that not pausing could potentially cause us money or even harm. Apparently, when geese waddle across your lane it is ample cause.

One driver didn't see the birds and decided to pull into the emergency lane to go around the cluster of stopped vehicles. My heart skipped a beat. He was headed directly toward our squatty northern visitors with an annoyed look on his face. Didn't he realize that there had to be a good reason for the other cars to be stopped? Didn't he understand that rushing to Target or McDonalds or wherever he was going wasn't a *real* emergency according to official traffic codes? He swerved at the last minute, one wheel going up on the grass to avoid disaster. I guess he finally did see the geese after all.

Meanwhile, like an office virus, the thoughtless driver's impatience was spreading quickly to others. Several cars turned their wheels, edging into the open lane in hopes of rushing on to their own un-emergencies. Luckily, at that very moment, the last earth bound goose stepped up from the road onto the curb, swishing its tail end and glancing back unconcerned at the steel beasts sitting in the street.

As I took a closer look, it appeared that these four geese were the last to arrive at a small goose convention being held in the parking lot across from the shopping mall. The awkward but beautiful birds stood around the edges of the concrete lot, forming a perfect "flying friends rectangle" as the newcomers joined the crowd. There were at least twenty or so birds gathered, and the street crossing seemed to have had little to no effect on their celebration. A few of the geese never reached the parking area, for I saw them plopped instead for a rest on the soft green grass under the leafless trees.

The goose crossing intrigued me. Even though the cars had stopped, I considered it an aberration in our driving patterns rather than the norm. What would it be like, I wondered, to live in a small town where the objects in the road, especially those that were alive, were always more important than getting to wherever you were going? A place where things were more personal, where if you yelled at another driver about their poor motoring skills during lunch rush hour your mother would hear about it before dinner? A place where people thought it normal to see geese in the road and stop to let them cross? I felt a small thrill, as if I'd just seen a bright red sunset streaked across the sky or spotted a movie star from the other side of the road. It's exciting to imagine a world where we are recognized and take time to recognize others. It made me hope for something better for all of us.

I've decided that I love watching geese on a busy Atlanta street. What I don't love is the thought that I am often like the drivers who almost missed it all because they were rushing to a place that didn't really care when they arrived and wouldn't really add much to their lives once they did. They missed the miracle rushing to the mundane. Lord, remind me that the virus of impatience takes away more from my heart than just peace. It can take away the hope that springs from unexpected kindness.

Let me always be surprised enough by the unlikely to pause and let geese cross in improbable places.

Chapter 7

The Seventh Promise of Hope:
Hope and Purity

Hope grows when our hearts are Pure.
Hope grows when we let go of anger and fear. We hope
better when we unburden ourselves and believe we are who
God says we are, not who others say we are.

"Blessed are the pure in heart for they will see God."
Matthew 5:9

JUST LIKE PETER

What's most constant about life is the way it is always changing. We expect change. We know that rivers will rise, ocean tides will ebb and seasons will change. It's a pretty sure bet that the stock markets will go up and then they will go back down again. We can guess that opinions will vary and moods will fluctuate. Some changes are a little more surprising. The revival of 1970's fashion, including big polka dots and bright pink and orange stripes caught me by surprise. After all, I wasn't that fond of it the first time around so I'm having a bit of a hard time with its resurrection.

People are no exception to this rule of change. They fluctuate just like the tides and fashion and the stock market. This is not news. All I need to do is look in the mirror to confirm this theory. The way I feel varies from day to day, the way I look alters based on the amount of sleep I get or the mood my hair is in, and my behavior can sometimes transform from normal to what is officially known as a little squirrelly.

So why does the inconsistency of others come as a surprise to me? Why don't I expect the unexpected, revel in the unanticipated, look forward to the bewildering? Instead of luxuriating in the constant of change, I find myself both startled and a little put out when life takes sudden turns. Like a disco ball slinging out dazzling patterns of light, my emotions react and can sometimes throw my heart into a seemingly useless whirl. When I am in this state, nothing looks as it should. I'd like to just accept the unexpected and move on. So, in an effort to better understand why I don't embrace the obvious, I've turned to scripture. You may be surprised to know that I find many characters with flaws similar to my own there.

Peter is a good example. You know, Simon Peter in the Bible. Peter covered the entire spectrum of action and emotion in his appearances in the New Testament. One day he was the first of the apostles to understand that Jesus was the Messiah. It was a revelation from God himself! The very next moment he was the bearer of very poor advice for Jesus and sharply corrected by Him. Peter was often a blunderer. He jumped out of a boat, walking across the water to hold onto Jesus. He's the only one you know; the only one of the apostles who wanted to be with Jesus enough to walk on the storm tossed waters to get to him. Just as he was getting close to his goal, he looked away, got scared and began to sink. Who wouldn't? Nevertheless, after the first few steps couldn't he just have held on until he reached his target? Why jump out of the boat at all if he was considering the hazards of the tossing waves? He hadn't studied the risks or considered carefully before he launched himself from the boat. It wasn't his style to delay action in order to ponder things. He jumped first, thought later.

Peter bragged that he would never desert Jesus and to prove it he cut off an ear of one of the men who came to arrest Him in Gethsemane's garden. Then he joined all the other apostles and ran for his life. One of his biggest flaws was that this big burly fisherman was easily overwhelmed by emotion. When he risked, he risked it all. When he ran away, he ran at full speed. One moment he was stepping up to protect the One he loved, the next cursing and swearing that he did not know Him at all. Peter really was quite a character. I'm thinking we might have been related.

Unlike me, some people can't relate to Peter's impetuousness. They take measured steps. They research and read and think and weigh options and only after great consideration do they move. But some of us jump. We tend to run towards those we love without considering whether we'll be swamped by the waves around them. We speak up quickly to share the love of God, telling others how knowing Christ has awakened our deepest heart. We sing loudly in church and get excited when we pray and know that God is alive and well and very interested in this world and its inhabitants. Then, just as quickly, we run from the unexpected, forget who we are, and forget also the power of the One we love. We rush—and our emotions, which energize us in our best moments, can crush us in our bad ones. Oh, we are learning to do it better, to slow it down and trust more. Still we can't seem to change how quickly our feelings turn to smiles or tears, faith or fear.

What I like about Jesus is that He knows all this about me and He accepts in advance those times when I will blow it. How do I know this? He knew it about Peter, didn't he? Jesus wasn't surprised by Peter's inconsistency. As a matter of fact, He made sure to tell Peter before it happened what he would do when it came to crunch time.

Jesus told Peter he would be among the first to share the good news of mankind's redemption and to build a living church. He also told Peter that he would deny Him. I like that Jesus was clear on exactly when and where these denials would occur so Peter would be sure to recognize the exact moment when things were nose diving. When that rooster crowed Peter immediately knew what he'd done. Apparently he needed an announcement from the animal kingdom that trumpeted the very moment of his betrayal.

It was a notable moment in mankind's history. It was a turning point for Peter. More than that, Peter needed to know that God had recognized the mess before it ever happened. His flaws, his worst moments, were known and accepted by God before they ever occurred.

After the resurrection, Jesus showed up on a shoreline to speak with Peter again. Three times He asked Peter, *"Do you love me?"* Each time Peter replied saying, *"You know that I love you, Lord!"* (John 21:15-18, NIV) In these three statements of love did Peter sense God releasing him from his previous three denials? Heaven's rhythm was breaking the power of his past and creating a future direction for Peter and those he would bless.

There's more. Peter's weren't small offenses to be easily dismissed. When he denied Jesus, it was the deepest kind of betrayal from a close friend. How it must have hurt to have your sworn protector turn away at the moment of your greatest need! At least the other disciples didn't swear to be faithful before they ran for cover. But Jesus had expected and accepted it all before it ever happened. God had provided grace for that moment in Peter's life during his acknowledgement of it. He had also encouraged Peter in advance.

So here is the question. Can I take what I know about the flaws of others, both present and future, and accept them in advance? Can I assume that the only constant with other humans is some degree of inconsistency? If I can admit that life holds some turns in the road ahead, I can use my emotions differently.

I once attended a class on personal safety. The teacher advised us all to decide in advance what we would do if caught in a dangerous situation.

"What would you do if someone tried to abduct you from a public parking lot?" he asked, looking at each of us in turn.

Then he shared some statistics with us regarding parking lot crimes and challenged us to decide in advance. Would we fight our assailants in the parking lot or save our energy for resistance at a second location? His advice was that whatever we did, we shouldn't wait for the emergency to think about it. Making a decision in the moment of calamity ensures that the flashing strobe light of emotion will be affecting your ability to think clearly. Decide now and you will act automatically on what your heart and head know is best for you when things don't go well. After you decide, rehearse or practice your decision. By the way, I'm not an expert on personal safety, but I'm fighting to stay out of that van the very first time!

This is what I want to do better in my relationship with God. Why wait until the crisis has blossomed and it's too late to think? I've already noted that things are pretty sure to get out of control at some point along the way. Why not decide to trust Him now? There are some things I know will happen. I will be disappointed. I will disappoint. Even though I am a "jumper" by nature, I can determine in advance where to jump. I can decide to expect the unexpected and to accept the unacceptable. It is only a small step from acceptance to forgiveness and letting go. Once that happens, there is a lot more room in my heart for other things to grow, like hope.

Now I guess I just need some practice. I'm picturing one of those tricky situations in my mind and I'm seeing myself trust, letting the power of my emotions strengthen the bonds of my faith. I'm far from perfect so try not to judge if you see me on a bad day. As a matter of fact, why don't you decide right now to give me, or whoever you run across today who isn't quite holding it all together, a little bit of a break or even a hug or a prayer. Surprise them.

Meanwhile, I am hoping for the best for all of us.

THIS OLD HOUSE

(This story is dedicated to my Aunt Mana, who loved me by showing her interest and absolute delight in who I was and what I did)

My aunt moved into an assisted living care facility when she was 82 years old. She loved it there, especially when a World War II veteran who had parachuted into Germany started courting her. We were all thrilled with the move, except maybe my cousins. They were responsible for getting rid of what was left in the house where my aunt had lived for the past fifty years. They called and asked us if we'd like to go through her household items and furniture to see if there was anything we might want. If it were me I'd have been crossing my fingers, hoping to see a stampede of relatives swarming over the place carrying off items only *they* could treasure, leaving the house shining like a plate licked clean by a hungry puppy. I actually think their motives were much more generous than that. An antique dealer was scheduled to come later in the week to identify and price valuable items, so they had given us first dibs on any potential treasures.

Deciding that my aunt needed the proceeds from the sale of her things more than I needed more furniture, I declined the offer. Nevertheless, I asked my mother about it.

"Was there anything you wanted from your sister's house? Was there anything of hers or your mother's left there that was valuable?" I asked her.

In mom's opinion there was only one item worth keeping, a table from the early 20th century passed down to my aunt by my grandmother. Because the table wasn't designed in a style that fit in with my mother's other belongings, she decided not to go get it. Both the value and the trouble of going through my aunt's belongings would fall to her own children. By the time I knew about the table, it was too late to tell my cousins to grab it and keep it. Hopefully the antique dealer knew its value and said something to them.

Imagine that. Only one thing worth keeping as a legacy, one item valuable enough to hold on to as a remembrance of another generation. A house full of bits and pieces and just one of them that provided a connection that was meaningful to my mother. Yet, like my aunt, most of us hold onto all kinds of belongings and then, when we have to move on and can no longer physically sort through the debris of our lives, we depend on those we love to do the work for us.

Now don't get me wrong. My aunt had other legacies she left to us, other things of value that live in hearts instead of houses. For me, it was her joy and encouragement. In her nursing home, I often found my aunt enthusiastically pushing her new boyfriend around in his wheelchair. She was half blind from macular degeneration and he was unable to walk after too many jumps out of airplanes in World War II. So he provided the eyes, telling her which way to go, and she provided the power. Her nurses loved her. Who wouldn't?

Whenever I came to visit, I always brought a new story I was writing because she was an avid reader and one of my biggest fans.

"Want to hear a new story?" I would ask, hoping to find a willing audience for my thoughts.

"Oh, yes," she would exclaim and we'd head outside to the little area in the middle of the U shaped building. I would open the computer and read as long as she would listen.

In the middle of one story about a cat who got locked out of the garage, she called out, "Oh, no! You didn't close the door did you?" Later in the reading of the same story when the cat's litter of kittens appeared lost in the woods she asked, full of concern, "Where were the babies?" She was so involved in each reading that she just couldn't contain herself.

She seemed to jump inside the stories and get lost in them. When I finished, she would sigh first, real big and breathy with a sort of surprise as she exhaled and then cry out in her throaty voice, "That's just beautiful, Jan!" My aunt gave me things that can't be bought and sold and that still take up room in my heart today.

But I am getting sidetracked here. Let me go back to my aunt's house, where fifty years of living had been left behind. What if instead of holding on to so many items, she had cleaned them out on a regular basis and left only the beautiful or useful items behind, as she did with things of the heart? Or maybe a better question would be what if you and I cleaned out the unneeded, unwanted items in our lives on a regular basis? What if every once in a while we wandered through the attics of our minds and cleared out anything that was collecting dust or just crowding up the space in our hearts? What if we determined that we wouldn't leave that job to those who are left behind—all that sorting through old family grudges or unresolved bitterness at previous injustices from those we once loved? We could choose to go through the clutter and get some sunlight and fresh air in our hearts.

What would happen to us if we did do some internal spring cleaning?

We know what happens when we collect pain and anger and leave it around for others to stumble over. We hand down prejudice and judgment without a second thought. We leak our bad feelings over the pavement of our family's lives like blackened oil from a broken car. It leaves a stain that's hard to remove.

It's not just the legacy and burden of what we leave behind either. It's the agility of our hearts, or lack of it, that is at stake. When we hold on to things they tend to take hold of us. There comes a time when we may want to let go but what we've held on to doesn't want to let go of us. It is very hard to hope when your mind is filled with all the wrongs done to you. Hope grows more easily when you make room for it in your heart.

I learned this principle in a very odd way. In my twenties someone I cared for hurt me deeply. One day, as I was driving home from work, this person came to mind. Following close behind was my anger. As I was recalling this person's flaws and the wounds they had inflicted, a scripture flashed across my mind.

"*Forgive and you will be forgiven*." (Luke 6:37b, NIV) I hadn't been thinking about God or scripture or forgiveness so I was a bit taken aback.

"Lord," I called out from behind the wheel of my car. "Surely you aren't talking to me! What do I have to be forgiven for?"

After quickly reconsidering where we could go with that line of questioning, I decided not to pursue it. Instead, I countered by reminding myself and God of the miles of wreckage left behind in my life, and my children's lives, by the one who really needed some forgiveness. That person wasn't me. The one in need didn't care about receiving my forgiveness and I was sure they weren't giving any thought to it on the way home from wherever they worked.

The thought that I should forgive came to me three times. Each time I argued its validity. When the scripture flashed across my mind for the last time it occurred to me that maybe I should pay attention. I didn't feel up for what I was being asked to do but I felt compelled to try anyway. Was forgiveness of this kind even possible?

Deciding to at least go through the motions, I responded to what appeared to be a clear directive from heaven's play book. Making it clear to God that I wasn't feeling the love, or forgiveness, I asked for His help. Then I pictured this person's face in my mind and imagined myself holding a rubber stamp in my hand. On it was the word *forgiven*. With more intensity than was probably required, I began stamping. Over and over I pictured myself stamping the word *forgiven* on his face until I felt my own heart unclenching, the roots of bitterness releasing their hold in the soil of my own soul.

It was an unusual roadway interaction, I admit. People have told me that there is no way I could have released my enemy and been released myself that simply. All I can say is that when all that stamping was done, when there was no room left on the picture in my brain and no anger left in my heart, I felt a relief that I couldn't have conceived earlier. It was exhilarating.

That release, with a few tune ups over the years, has taken me far from the prison of my anger against that person. The resulting freedom has left me hoping I can forgive again when I need to and that others can forgive me as well.

Maybe the best part of the whole experience is that the clinging oil stain of anger and bitterness, at least in this instance, didn't have the opportunity to darken the hearts of my children. If I had kept the anger and let it grow, it almost certainly would have been passed down to them. Whatever else they have to deal with when I'm gone, it won't be this. Hopefully, something more valuable is growing in their hearts instead.

I hope you will give it a try, even if it seems impossible or feels improbable. Let it go. Whatever is cluttering up your heart, forgive the deed and the person who did it and move on. Don't be afraid to ask for help if you need some. I'm betting there are more rubber stamps in your heavenly Father's keeping if you want one.

Then after you have let it go, thank your aunt, or mom, or dad or whoever has been a cheerleader in your life. No use clearing out all that room in your heart without filling it up with something better. Why not saturate it with a little gratitude?

That will keep you hoping.

MY SISTER AND I

"Mama was shaking real bad last night," my sister Mundy said. "I know because I was holding her hand."

I looked at her, my eyebrows drawing together as I thought back to our evening. I knew Mundy was concerned with my mother's declining health. We all were. It's hard to watch someone you love in a long struggle with something you know they cannot beat, short of a miracle. Parkinson's was the diagnosis the doctors had given us a few years ago and we had watched the ups and downs of mom's battle--getting on medication, getting the dosage right, adjusting it continually as time and the effects of the disease marched on. Despite all the help of modern medicine, mother's good days were fewer and her off days were increasing. I think as much as anything her battle was against the force of lethargy, a kind of physical and mental gravity that slowed my mother's movements and mind. Half the battle is just staying in the battle and when you can't find the energy to get out of your chair, it's hard to pick up your sword and fight.

The news to me in all this wasn't that mom had been shaking but that Mundy felt her shaking last night. My sister had been on one side of my mother while I was on the other. Like bookends keeping a priceless edition standing, we held her between us. We went down the long hallway to the elevator and then out to the car, having optimistically left her walker in her room. We encouraged her to bring her cane instead. Mundy held on to the side of mom that was free, while I put my hand loosely on her back so as not to impede the arm using the cane.

That was the difference then. There wasn't any shaking on mom's left side where I stood. The arm with the cane moved slowly but steadily, forward, back, forward, with each foot obediently following behind. Where my arm rested on her back, I felt her labored progress but no shaking.

I was tempted to ask my sister if she'd been mistaken, to tell her that all was well on the left side. Could she have misinterpreted what was going on with the right? That was ridiculous of course. I walked with my mother enough days to know her symptoms well. It was just that our experience that evening had been so different, all because of our placement no more than a foot away from each other on opposite sides of our mother.

Funny, isn't it? I realized our whole lives had been a little like that, maybe even more so with our father than with our mother. I was the second in a family of four children, born when my father was young enough and still strong enough to both love and bully us. Mundy was the last of the four children, born when my mother was forty. By then my father's asthma had grown to a gale force in both his life and ours, taking all his effort and breath during the days and his peace at night. When I was young, he was able to pour both his will and deep love into forming the vessel that became my life. When Mundy was young he had little will left to pour so she received his simple adoration on his good days. On his bad days his effect on her was nominal. By this time, my mother had learned to ignore my father rather than try to please him and she taught my sister to do the same.

I had no such defense from his great ambition and the criticism he thought would motivate me to greatness. On the other hand, I did not need any defense from his warm father's love. These were the two sides of the man who first taught me about love.

While I have often thought of what his struggles left me, I didn't understand until I was much older what it cost him to love me so. I was oblivious to what happened to his body when he climbed on a horse and rode side by side with me on the ragged trail behind the public stable. He never mentioned the allergies triggered by these rides or the ensuing spike in his war with asthma once we dismounted. Even the simple evenings when I sought a midnight refuge from my fears in my parents' bed were hard on him. I never considered that on those mornings when I saw him bending his arm, a hand resting on the small of his back, he was massaging away the pain left after a night sleeping with a small child nestled in the crook of his back. I guess he knew somehow that sleeping near him was the only way I could defeat the dream monsters that haunted my sleep. With dad I was safe from the monsters in the closet and in my dreams, but I was not safe from the power of his wishes for my life.

Mundy was safe from both once my mother taught her to stop listening during the hurtful times, at least for that period in her life. It would take her years to listen to any unpleasant thing, even the warning bells meant to direct her away from the ragged edges of life toward safety. She had learned to still almost all alarms, both gentle and sharp in order to drown out my father's anger and pain. What she did hear from him was love, but it was an aging love sometimes given from the distance of exhaustion.

So there we were— Mundy on one side of dad with me on the other; me on one side of mom, Mundy on the other. We were children who were loved and molded on opposite sides of our parents' lives. Eventually I would discover that my life was fuller when my sister and I lashed together the puzzle pieces of our understanding and shared what we learned on the sides we were given. My perception was not reality, as many claim, but only one part of reality, incomplete on its own, in need of another's experience.

Even the sum of these fragments, which we pieced together like broken glass, formed a somewhat uneven picture of our parents. We experienced more as we grew and those later experiences would leave their imprint as well.

In my early twenties, while living in Florida and learning about God, I began to write to my father. I missed much of God in my early church life, living within the lines of religious rules and only occasionally experiencing the God they supposedly represented. I stopped believing altogether somewhere along the way. Then, unexpectedly, the God I had missed in childhood reached into my heart, causing it to breathe in new rhythms with the joy of His spirit. This changed the direction of my young adult life and I shared those experiences with my father.

He must have thought about it before responding because he waited a while to write back. When he did I was surprised to learn that a priest in the confessional spoke to him in similar terms as I, offering him the opportunity to "accept Christ in his heart." In the church life of my childhood, this was not the normal conversation of cathedral penances.

To my surprise he responded to this invitation, accepting the One whom he sought in his private heart for years. Dad found a real and personal dialogue with a God who influenced him in life but who, until that time, he had not allowed to hold him. I remembered this after he died when I found the letters I had written to him in his dresser drawer. Mom said he had saved every one.

Mundy and I carry different parts of him; she his blue eyes, I his prominent chin, she his love of teaching, I his desire for justice. We also carry his weaknesses—both physical and emotional—but they seem to have given way, in some measure, to the strength he imparted. Both of us have his soft heart and keen mind and when I look at my sister I see a legacy of beauty and imperfection, of strength and struggle.

In our generation we have found sooner than my parents the Love that changes all. It has helped us to find the best of our father in us.

Thank you, daddy. Thank you, mom.

We will hold you up as long as we can and hopefully offer back to you some of what you have given us.

Chapter 8

FINAL THOUGHTS

"I remember my affliction and my wandering, the bitterness and the gall. I well remember them and my soul is downcast within me. Yet this I call to mind and therefore I have hope. Because of the Lord's great love we are not consumed, for his compassions never fail. They are new every morning, great is your faithfulness. I say to myself, 'the Lord is my portion. Therefore I will wait for him.' The Lord is good to those whose hope is in him." Lamentations 3:19-25

"I think there are two types of hope," Chris said.

He looked at me, smiled, and took another bite of his enchilada. Our lunch was the result of what some might call a random meeting after a speaking engagement of mine with a local job networking group. Chris had come to the meeting at the suggestion of a friend, the meeting's organizer. He wasn't looking for a job but his friend thought we should meet and she's in the business of connecting people who have things in common. So he came and we met. As things have it, within a very short time Chris was looking for a job himself. Not long after that, another friend of mine's company had an opening that happened to match Chris's qualifications and well, let's just say it was a story with a happy ending. More and more lately I find that the word "random" is out of place in my life's vocabulary.

On this day, Chris and I were having lunch to catch up on things. Chris has a special needs son, wheelchair bound for life, as well as two other teenage children and a wonderful wife. When you listen to him talk, you can practically see the light shining from him. He is creative and bright and, well, hopeful.

As it happened, I had taken a week off to put together some thoughts on hope. Having sensed that hope was emerging as a theme in my life, that just as some people are drawn to play sports or a musical instrument, to fix car engines or enforce the law, I was drawn to hope and to share that hope with others. Still, I wasn't sure I quite knew how to define it. As soon as I began to write about hope, I found myself asking what exactly it was. Was it wishing? Was it a heavenly GPS, guiding us to our best lives? Or was it more like the fuel in the gas tank on the drive through our existence here on earth? I thought I should ask a few more questions before I decided to talk about it to others.

So, while Chris shared some of his story with me, I asked him how he would define hope. I try to keep it real by asking those who've lived through hard times why there is a reason to hope. Chris' son is unable to do the simplest task for himself and will be living with Chris and his wife for life. Chris' job, the one my contact offered him seven months ago, was a temporary assignment and is ending soon. The current economic recession is still very real and unemployment is at its highest level in almost 30 years. So, once again, Chris was looking for his next opportunity. Between mouthfuls of his favorite Mexican food, he shared some thoughts with me.

"One type of hope is a sort of wishing that we all do. We say 'I hope it won't rain today' or 'I hope traffic is good', or 'I hope I live to a ripe old age.' For some of us that is the totality of our hope. But there is something more. It is anchored in God."

Chris looked at me, paused for a moment to gather his thoughts and then continued.

"God's hope is altogether different from "wishing" hope. Here's how it works. Before I believed in God, I hoped for good weather and a long life. Now that have a relationship with God, I hope for good weather and a long life. This is fine as far as it goes. In my previous way of thinking, I was disappointed when my hopes weren't fulfilled and I didn't get what I wanted. But with hope that is centered in God, it isn't just about the circumstances. The circumstances surrounding me may still stink but I am not disappointed. The object of my hope changes from looking for a happy, comfortable life to looking for a life where I am walking with God. Sure, I continue to hope in His promises. He always makes good on them; always does, always will. But sometimes He answers in ways I would not expect."

"The best hope", Chris emphasized," is anchored in God himself, in His very presence in our lives, not necessarily in a change of our circumstances. It doesn't matter what we face because we know He is in every part of our story. When we hope in God, we find a whole new meaning of hope," Chris said.

Chris should know. He has hoped in God and His loving presence through some pretty tough times. During his family's journey, when the news was devastating and continued to get worse, they learned to hold on to their heavenly Father, whose sight is unaffected by the fog of our lives. They learned that what they needed to do was hope and trust in His proficiency, not their own. When they could not control the outcome, they could still hope in Him. After all, when you know how the story ends you can breathe deeper and live fuller.

According to Chris, we hope in God's love and ability, not in our circumstances. When your hope is anchored in Him, it is secure.

Bibliography/Notes

1. Cohen, L. (Composer). (1992). Anthem..The Future. [L. Cohen, Performer] On *The Essential Leonard Cohen*.

2. Martin Luther King, J. (n.d.). *I have a dream speech*.

3. Havel, V. (1986, tr. 1990). *Disturbing the Peace*.

4. Bevere, J. *Extraordinary; The Life You're Meant to Live*. Waterbrook Press eBooks.

5. Covey, S. R. (1990). *The Seven Habits of Highly Effective People*. First Fireside Edition, Simon and Schuster.

6. Young, W. P. (2007). *The Shack*. Newbury Park, CA: Windblown Media.

7. *The Holy Bible, New International Version*. (1996). Grand Rapids, MI: Zondervan Bible Publishers.

For a ***free hope story download***, a look at our new ***hope blog***, and the chance to upload your own ***hope thoughts*** go to:

<u>www.YourHopeGrows.com</u>